Forty Years in Hollywood

By the Same Authors
Hill of Life: The Story of Joseph Trumpeldor
The Faces of Israel

Forty Years in Hollywood:

Portraits of a Golden Age

Roman Freulich and Joan Abramson

CASTLE BOOKS ★ NEW YORK

This Edition Published by Arrangement
with A. S. Barnes & Co., Inc.

Printed in the United States of America

For Katherine, with love

Contents

Acknowledgments 9

Introduction 11

1 "Jesus Himself only gets $75 a week" 15

2 "Carl Laemmle Presents . . ." 64

3 "Put some money on Republic" 114

4 "Someone is click clicking away" 155

Index 199

Acknowledgments

The authors wish to acknowledge the kind assistance received from David Lipton, vice president of Universal Studios, and from Mildred Simpson, head librarian of the Motion Picture Academy of Arts and Sciences, as well as from her fine staff.

Introduction

In Hollywood the make-believe has been entangled with the real for so many years that it is sometimes difficult for those who have been involved to separate the two. Stories are told and retold, embroidered and embellished; and the actual sometimes slips into the realm of the apocryphal.

Yet, each of the stories we relate in this book has some kind of reality. Many are incidents experienced or witnessed by the photographer, who spent over forty years in the film industry. Others were passed on to him by his friends and acquaintances in the film world. But all have an authenticity—all are true to the spirit of Hollywood during its most flamboyant and narcissistic age.

Today we hear a great deal about the new kind of film maker. Somehow, we are told, he is more inventive and more creative than his predecessor. And, we are assured, he has far fewer hangups than his predecessor. I wonder if the children of today's film makers will think that this is true. Or will they, perhaps, look back over almost a century of film making and see a continually changing and evolving medium that exhibits no striking breaks between the "old" and the "new."

Certainly when one thinks back over the forty years spanned by this book, one sees constant change as a major factor in the growth of the film industry.

Mr. Freulich himself is typical of that change. His own career was one of innovation and creativity. He came to Hollywood during the early 1920s, after serving in the British army during World War I. Like all photographers at that time, he worked with the bulky cameras and tripods that made the profession, of necessity, one for only young and healthy men. But ten years later he was experimenting with the use of the tiny 35 millimeter camera for professional, on-set photography. And he was experimenting so successfully that he won international recognition for his work. It wasn't until 25 years later that the rest of the industry caught up with Freulich, but now neither film nor magazine photographers would think of working with large cameras on most of their assignments.

Like many of the other creative people of Hollywood, Freulich was never satisfied with the old ways of doing things. He was constantly experimenting, constantly trying out new techniques and new materials and devices. He was one of the first Hollywood photographers to perfect techniques of color photography and throughout his career he remained one of the industry's top color photographers.

His innovative urges even encouraged him to

11

venture into the world of motion picture production and writing. During the 1930s, Freulich became one of the first of Hollywood's avant-garde film makers. He wrote, produced and photographed a film called *The Prisoner,* which was considered one of the best of the early attempts at psychological interpretation on the screen. He also wrote, produced and photographed *Broken Earth,* the first film to feature a Negro in a starring role. The short film, which starred Clarence Muse, was an attempt to show the Negro as a human being instead of as the mincing, shuffling clown he was made to seem in the usual Hollywood productions of the time.

Freulich also turned his talents to one of the first books on the film industry. With Ray Hoadley he wrote *How They Make a Motion Picture,* which was for years the only book available on Hollywood film making techniques.

During those years he continued to perfect his own special art. His articles on portrait and pinup photography and on the advances in photographic technique appeared in numerous magazines and newspapers. His photographs appeared inside and on the covers of *Life, Look, Newsweek, International Photographer,* and a dozen other magazines. He won awards in international and national exhibits and brought home four Academy Awards.

The photographs included here are only a small sample of Mr. Freulich's work. Looking through them will undoubtedly call up many memories for followers of the motion picture industry. They are a remarkable display of photographic talent and creativity from one man's remarkable career in the film industry.

Forty Years in Hollywood

1

"Jesus Himself only gets $75 a week"

In the past few years Hollywood has produced its most self-laudatory exhibit on that once rival medium, television. The nation watches while praise is lavished on the film industry by the film industry—while the Academy Awards are presented to the industry by the industry. And while watching it is easy enough to be convinced that Hollywood believes its own extravagant and self-created image.

But there has always been a saving streak of irreverence in film folk and there has always been the ability within the industry to laugh at its own creations. These qualities have been with Hollywood from the beginning—from the days when, in fact, there was very little respect for actors and acting. They have been with Hollywood from the days when actors were commodities to be purchased as cheaply as possible in order to assure profits as large as possible; from the time before anyone imagined that an extravagant image was necessary to sell a star and thus to sell a film.

Actors came to films almost as an afterthought when the novelty of moving shadows on a screen no longer attracted audiences. And when actors did come they added new problems to those the producers already had.

One of these early problems was a result of the crude state of the art of film makeup. Stage makeup, which could be exaggerated in a large theater, looked grotesque on the screen. And for a long while, before the techniques of film makeup were refined, producers fell back upon typecasting as a substitute.

Among these early silent-screen producers were Abe and Julius Stern, two brothers who were best known for their Baby Peggy film series. The brothers soon grew tired of their series of insipid comedies and decided to produce a truly artistic film. It would be a true spectacle, something they would both be remembered by: a movie based on the life of Jesus.

In order to do justice to the various characters, the brothers purchased a large copy of Leonardo daVinci's *Last Supper* and began to sign up actors to fit the great painter's concept of the Disciples. Before long the script was completed, the sets were built and dressed and the cast had been selected—with the single exception of an actor to play the part of Judas.

The two brothers had their staff search all over Hollywood, but they could not come up with a single actor who looked the part. As a last resort their combination bookkeeper, assistant and casting director decided to attend every play in the Los Angeles area to see if a proper Judas could be found among stage actors.

After two weeks of looking at live performances, the casting director attended a performance given by a well known and highly respected road company. He could barely contain his excitement through the performance, for at long last he had found the man he was looking for—a man who not only looked the part of Judas, but who could act as well.

After the performance he hurried backstage and pleaded with the actor to come to the studio the next morning. The actor, who did not want to appear overly anxious, at last agreed. But to keep up the appearance of being unconcerned he arrived at the studio one half hour after the appointed time. He was immaculately dressed, from his black derby to his patent leather shoes, and he carried a beautiful ivory handled cane in his gloved hand.

The two brothers, who considered themselves shrewd businessmen above everything else, immediately recognized that he was perfect for the role. But they were not going to let the actor know how badly they needed him.

"Too bad," mused Abe, slowly rising from his desk and walking around to inspect the actor from behind as if he were inspecting a new piece of office furniture. "Too bad. We've been told you're green at this game. But maybe, just maybe you could learn. You look fairly intelligent."

"I don't know," commented Julius. "No experience, absolutely none. Can we trust a project this important to someone with no film experience. Stage plays are all very well, but. . . . After all, it's our money he'd be learning on."

After five minutes of this, the two brothers realized that the seasoned actor who sat before them was still completely cool and absolutely unimpressed so they quickly changed tactics.

"We'll make you famous," said Abe.

"And rich, too," added Julius.

"We'll do for you what we did for Erich von Stroheim," shouted Abe.

"Absolutely!" echoed Julius.

And so they went on, enthusiastically lauding their own value to the already secure actor and mentioning everything except money.

When they had finally worn down to the last possible topic of conversation the actor coolly asked what they expected to pay him.

"Seventy-five dollars a week. And for five full weeks!" said Abe, still gushing enthusiasm.

"Seventy-five dollars?" the actor echoed. For the first time he allowed some emotion to show through his cool façade. He got up angrily, plunked his derby onto his head, tucked his cane under one arm and began pulling on his suede gloves. "Seventy-five dollars? Sorry, gentlemen, I'm not interested."

The two brothers cut him off. Abe grabbed the actor by the arm while Julius headed for the door to bar his exit. They deluged him once again with reminders of the fame that would come his way if he appeared in their film.

"They'll know your name . . . even in Africa," Julius assured him.

"I haven't got any ambition to appear in films," the actor replied. "Besides, I'd be giving up a long run play for five weeks' work. And I never work for less than $125 a week."

With that the actor tried once again to make his way to the door. But Julius had not given up his station there. He stood firmly in the actor's path.

Finally the actor cried out in desperation, "What do you want from me? I'm simply not interested. I just won't work for that salary. Can't you understand that?"

Abe at last sensed his defeat. Once again he grabbed the actor firmly by the arm. He steered him back toward his big desk. "All right, all right," he said. He shuffled papers about his desk in exasperation and then began scratching changes in the already prepared contract he had before him.

"All right, so we'll give you your $125," Abe

moaned. "But I want you to know, Mr. Broadway Actor, I want you to know that Jesus himself only gets $75 a week!"

* * *

In spite of experiences that were sometimes damaging to their egos, stage actors eventually came flocking to Hollywood in the hopes of enhancing both name and pocketbook with a Hollywood film or two.

Among those who were enamored of the idea of becoming film stars was Maurice Schwartz, who was already a leading star of the Yiddish stage, manager of his own theater company, and an acknowledged master actor. Schwartz had kept an eye on actors from the Yiddish theater who had gone to Hollywood. Among these actors was Paul Muni, a man whose acting ability, Schwartz felt, was infinitely inferior to his own. Yet Muni had become a Hollywood star and with his stardom had come wealth and a worldwide reputation. Schwartz soon became convinced that the Yiddish theater was too narrow a vehicle for his talents. He would go to Hollywood and he would become a star. Obviously it could not be difficult, for even Paul Muni had been able to accomplish that end.

Shortly before he was due to appear in Hollywood in a traveling version of the play *Yoshe Kalb,* Schwartz hired a Hollywood agent. A combination of his talent and his agent's connections, he reasoned, could not be beaten.

The agent, in fact, did manage to convince Louis B. Mayer to attend a performance of the Schwartz play. Mayer was impressed and he had no doubts at all that his studio could make use of Schwartz. Biographical films were in vogue at the time and Warner Brothers, with Paul Muni under contract, had no competition in the field. With Schwartz, Mayer was sure he could give Warner Brothers more than enough competition. He sent an aid to talk with Schwartz after the play and to ask him to come to the studio the following day to sign a long-term contract.

It seemed that everything had gone according to plan—and with the greatest of ease. Schwartz, in fact, signed a contract that provided him with a good salary as well as with the right to reject scripts. It was that clause, however, that later caused Schwartz a good deal of trouble.

When the engagement of *Yoshe Kalb* ended, Schwartz disbanded his troupe. Most of the actors returned to New York, but a few stayed in Hollywood in hopes of getting film jobs. Schwartz was called in and introduced to various producers and directors, among them an old New York acquaintance who was working as an assistant casting director.

The studio assigned a special publicity agent to Schwartz. Photos were made of him and appointments were set up for him to meet a number of newsmen and columnists who covered the Hollywood scene.

Everything was off to a promising start. It seemed that nothing could interfere with the film career of Maurice Schwartz.

But not long after he had been introduced to the Hollywood columnists, Schwartz had his first run-in with the studio. He was asked to do a film test, which would be made available to the various directors and producers who might have potential roles for him.

Schwartz decided to do the famous Shylock speech from *The Merchant of Venice.* On the day of the test, he arrived at the studio and found that the head of the makeup department was on hand to apply his makeup personally. But Schwartz was unhappy with the results. He stripped the makeup and began again, working as he had during his theater days.

The test scene went well. Schwartz was brilliant, and completely unperturbed by the camera. But when the film was developed, the closeups were ludicrous. The heavy theatrical makeup, which may have been perfect in a large theatre, was ridiculous on a large screen.

The test had been a complete waste of time and money. Studio executives viewed it and quickly decided that it had been a mistake to allow Schwartz the privileges of an experienced star. He would no longer be allowed to have his own way.

An executive was assigned to talk with Schwartz, and particularly to explain to him that in Hollywood union rules prohibited actors from applying their own makeup. Schwartz was warned that further infractions would be considered a breach of contract.

Schwartz had a second run-in with the studio when the time came to read his first script. He had suggested that the studio allow him to do a film version of a Russian play called *The Seven Who Were Hanged*. He considered the play a perfect vehicle for his own acting talents. But in spite of his efforts, the studio presented him with a different script. And Schwartz, who still felt quite secure in his position, refused to do any acting in that film.

Two months later, the studio called him in to view a French film that starred Harry Bauer. The studio had purchased the rights to an American version of the film and executives were considering it as the vehicle for Schwartz's first starring role.

The film was an impressive one, but once again Schwartz turned it down. He did not wish to appear in a remake of someone else's film. Once again he urged the executives to star him in *The Seven Who Were Hanged.*

With an already-signed contract and a would-be star who refused every script offered to him, studio executives allowed the weeks and months to slip by. Eventually they did not even bother sending scripts to Schwartz's home.

The appointments with columnists came to an end. The publicity agent was put to work elsewhere. And paychecks began to arrive by mail.

But Schwartz had not come to Hollywood merely to make money. He had come to act and to let the world see the talent that had been limited to the relatively small audience of the Yiddish theater.

Several months went by. Word came that the lease on his New York theater had been taken over by another company. Maurice Schwartz was rapidly become little more than a pleasant memory for Yiddish theater regulars.

Schwartz called together a small group of friends and acquaintances to discuss his problem. His mistake had been in insisting on the one play, *The Seven Who Were Hanged,* for his film debut. Now the problem was simply to get his name back in the news and in the minds of studio executives. Once that was done, he could convey his willingness to appear in a film of the studio's choosing.

The best way to get back in the news, they decided, was to throw a big party and invite all the top people from the studio.

The idea captured his enthusiasm immediately. He began to prepare for the big event. He arranged for the finest delicatessen in town to cater the food and he sent to New York for special orders of slivovitz and fine Yugoslavian wines. In fact, he became so engrossed in planning for the big night that he had little time left to talk with his friends. Several calls came to him from his old acquaintance, the assistant casting director at the studio, but Schwartz cut the man off with promises that he would return the call when things seemed less pressing. Whatever his old acquaintance wanted could wait. He wanted nothing, neither good news nor problems, to interfere with the plans for his party.

The night of the party finally arrived. For the first time since he arrived in Hollywood, his hillside mansion was open to the high and the mighty. Attendants waited to guide chauffeurs to parking places or to park cars for those few who were invited who had not yet reached prestigious enough positions to require chauffeurs. Maids waited to take hats and gloves and furs. Caterers waited to serve, bartenders to pour. And a gypsy band waited to play and sing for the guests.

Schwartz was superb in his role as host. He suggested fine liqueurs and wines, poured champagne, hurried maids around with platters of food to make sure no one went away hungry. He spent time with each guest, listened attentively, told his best jokes and then hurried on to the next guest—no one was going to feel slighted by the great actor that night.

At last a murmur passed through the crowd—

the guest of honor, Louis B. Mayer, had arrived. Schwartz rushed to greet him and the rest of his evening was spent hovering about the great man and entertaining him. Mayer seemed rather taciturn that evening. But he was required to say very little. He ate and drank and listened while Schwartz told anecdotes of his life as a New York actor.

In fact, Mayer seemed so appreciative that Schwartz allowed his hopes to rise once again. Instead of promising to make his film debut in any film the studio wished, he once more broached the subject of appearing in *The Seven Who Were Hanged.*

At last, when he was stuffed with food and awash with drink, Mayer began to talk. He assured Schwartz that his party had been fine, that he was a great actor and that he would think seriously about making *The Seven Who Were Hanged.*

Schwartz pressed the point again as his taciturn guest prepared to leave.

"Well, why not," came the answer. "See me at nine on Monday morning and we'll make it definite."

Schwartz went to bed a happy man. The rest of the weekend went much too slowly and on Monday he reported to the offices of Louis B. Mayer. The pretty receptionist asked him what he wanted.

"I've an appointment with the boss," he replied.

The girl looked puzzled. But she picked up her phone and called Mayer's private secretary. Then she turned to Schwartz.

"I'm sorry, Mr. Schwartz, you must be mistaken. Mr. Mayer isn't planning to come in this morning. I'm sure you've got the date mixed up."

In spite of his protests, the girl insisted that Mayer had not come in and had no intention of coming to the studio that morning.

At last Schwartz left. He fled to his home and placed a call to the publicist who had handled his introduction to the press when he had first been hired. The publicist tried to pacify him, and promised to look into the matter and to call him back.

When the call did come, the news was not good.

"I'm sorry," the publicist reported. "I guess you might as well know now as hang around. There isn't any intention around here of using you. At least not now. And I can't see when they will. I'm really sorry."

After a few days Schwartz recovered sufficiently to call another meeting of his friends. The assistant casting director who had been so anxious to talk to him before the party was there, but he hadn't the heart to talk any longer. The gloomy company decided that nothing could be gained by Schwartz's hanging around Hollywood. He should look into the possibility of canceling his contract and head back to New York while he still had some reputation left in the theater world.

Schwartz managed to settle with the studio. He was presented with a sizable check, packed his belongings, gave up the lease on his hillside mansion and retreated to New York. He was puzzled and disgusted by the strange people of Hollywood and glad to be back in the more familiar atmosphere of the theater world.

The assistant casting director never did have the heart to tell him—all the frantic calls before the Schwartz party were meant to warn him to change the date of the affair.

Louis B. Mayer had planned another party on the same evening—a huge party to be held at a Hollywood nightclub—a party to which most of the people Schwartz had invited would be going.

The assistant casting director had been unable to talk to his friend. Not wanting to see him hurt, and hoping Schwartz would appreciate the joke, he had made his own elaborate plans. He had rounded up all the doubles for actors and actresses who had been invited to the Schwartz party and asked them to come. And he had even convinced a studio tailor with a striking resemblance to Louis B. Mayer to come in the guise of the studio head. He had also collected personal favors owed him by studio grips and teamsters and had costumed them as chauffeurs and equipped them with studio cars for the event.

It had started as a joke and he had every intention of letting his friend know when things were going a little better for him. It would cheer him up, he felt, both at the time it was under way and later, when he would tell him how he had managed it.

And he had managed the whole ruse without being discovered—Schwartz had been too busy with his own plans and too intoxicated with his own success to admit the possibility that anything was amiss.

Years later, after he had returned to the Yiddish theater, Schwartz accepted a small part in the Warner Brothers film, *Mission to Moscow.* When the film came to the New York East Side, the heart of the Yiddish theater area, an astute theater manager placed Schwartz's name in huge letters on his marquee. Schwartz had at last become a movie star.

*   *   *

Actors were not the only ones treated with irreverence by the film industry. During the 1930s, Hollywood studios considered it an important prestige factor to have among their script writers one or two men who had achieved distinction in the field of literature. But they did not treat these men with any special kindness.

At Columbia Studios, where Harry Cohn presided in the head office, William Saroyan was hired to fill this role.

Cohn was a businessman first and foremost and he insisted upon the excellence of his ability to judge the potential box-office success of any script. He therefore maintained the policy that no film could go into production at Columbia until he had seen and approved the script.

The fact that Saroyan had best selling books to his credit did not impress Harry Cohn, for he did not read novels and rarely attended plays. What did impress Cohn, and impress him unfavorably, was that Saroyan could not write a script worthy of production. At last, in complete exasperation at Saroyan and the whole idea of hiring literary figures to write film scripts, Cohn

asked the studio legal department to pay off and get rid of "that Armenian rug peddler." He had thumbed through one after another of Saroyan's scripts and sent them back in disgust. Maintaining him on the payroll, Cohn felt, was a complete waste of studio funds.

Saroyan left the studio without showing any emotion. It did not seem too disturbing to him to be rejected by a man of Harry Cohn's literary judgment. But he was not ready to let the slur on his Armenian background go unnoticed.

Several months went by and at last Saroyan came to pay a visit to Harry Cohn. It was no easy matter for an ordinary man to get past the receptionist in Cohn's outer office. But William Saroyan was not an ordinary man and he had long been a favorite of secretaries and receptionists around the studio. The receptionist and Cohn's secretary convinced the studio head to see the writer for a few minutes.

Saroyan did not have much that he wanted to say. The day was cold and rainy and he had come into the office wearing an old trench coat. He began to unbutton it slowly as he entered Cohn's office.

"Good morning, Mr. Cohn," Saroyan said.

He finished unbuttoning his coat and whipped out a small oriental rug which had been hidden beneath it.

"I won't try to sell you any of my stories today, Mr. Cohn," Saroyan said. "I know you find them bad box-office material and unartistic as well. But I do wonder if you would be interested in this fine Armenian prayer rug."

Saroyan did not wait for the startled Cohn to reply. This time he wanted to reserve the last word for himself. He turned on his heel and left the head man sitting with his mouth open.

*   *   *

Saroyan was not alone in suffering from Harry Cohn's limited appreciation of literary talent.

Cohn, in fulfilling his role as sole judge of all scripts in the studio, once called in a studio writer who had completed a script that contained what the writer considered to be a rather moving scene inside a church. The writer stood in front of the head man while Cohn fussed and flipped through the pages of the script.

"You'll just have to go back over some of this. It's terrible," Cohn said.

"Where do you think it needs working over, sir?" the writer asked.

"Well, here—here for instance. This scene in the church. It's just phony. Nobody repeats prayers like that. Phony!"

"But sir," said the bemused writer, "that's the Lord's Prayer!"

"Lord's Prayer, Lord's shmayer," replied Cohn. "Fix it so people can understand it."

* * *

Producers and studio owners, Cohn among them, also came in for their share of irreverent treatment. But, unlike the actors, writers and technicians who often had to take the blows directly and nurse their bruised egos in public, the big men rarely came in for direct abuse. Most of it was behind the scenes and behind their backs—or even after their deaths.

When Harry Cohn died, the management of Columbia announced that the studio would be closed to allow all employees to attend his funeral. Since they were to receive their regular wages for the day, most employees assumed correctly that the request was, in fact, an order, and that they were serving as paid mourners.

Over 1500 people showed up at the cemetery for graveside ceremonies. One after another, the great personalities of Hollywood entered the cemetery grounds and paid their respects. One studio comic, at first astounded at the size of the crowd, soon pulled himself together and grinned, and then turned to his companions to whisper:

"See what I mean, fellows. When you give the people what they want, they're sure to come."

* * *

But talk of that kind could not always go un-

heard by the men against whom it was directed.

Cecil B. DeMille had a reputation for being a tyrant while he was directing a picture. He would strut about the stage with a megaphone, giving orders left and right and demanding immediate and untiring response. He rarely dismissed his crew when lunchtime came and he often continued to work into the evening hours without paying attention to time or to the exhaustion of his crew.

One day, while directing a scene from a crane suspended high above the floor of the stage, DeMille raised his megaphone and called for complete quiet. As usual, he got it. Everyone stopped what they were doing and stood waiting for DeMille's next words.

But there was, on this occasion, one extra in the crowd who had never before worked for DeMille. And just as DeMille was preparing to break the silence with his next order, he heard one small female voice.

"When is that sonofabitch gonna call lunch?" the extra asked.

Absolute silence took over again, but only for a moment. DeMille recovered himself, raised his megaphone to his mouth and shouted, "Lunch, everybody—one hour."

* * *

William Randolph Hearst came in for a slightly different kind of disrespect. He often frequented the studios to watch his paramour, Marion Davies, work.

One afternoon he walked onto a stage to await the close of the work day. Hearst approached the day watchman, whose job it was to keep tourists and strangers off the set while filming was going on.

"About when are they due to quit?" Hearst asked.

"About now, I'd say. It's five already." the watchman replied. Then he yawned, got up from his folding chair near the stage door and prepared to leave.

"Well," said the watchman, "my day is over

but your day is just starting. Good luck, I hope they clear out of your hair soon so maybe you can get a little sleep on the job."

The day watchman was in such a hurry to leave that he failed to notice the puzzled look Hearst gave him.

The next day a studio grip, who had overheard the exchange, told the watchman that the man he had mistaken for his night replacement was really William Randolph Hearst. The day watchman shrugged his shoulders and replied casually, "That's okay, I buy his paper."

* * *

Some of the disrespect heaped upon the big names was a natural outgrowth of jealousy or everyday griping common in any kind of work. Some of it, however, was fed and grew on the ineptitude or the pretensions of the big men themselves.

Pretentiousness was at the root of the lack of respect one producer brought upon himself in the early 1920s. The man had made several successful films when he decided that his own image needed smartening up. His success in a field that was supposed to be among the fine arts seemed to him to make it imperative that he himself be known as a man of good taste and broad knowledge in the fine arts.

He purchased a new and elegant home in Beverly Hills, paid a well-known interior decorator to furnish it with style and taste and sat back to await the results. But when the decorator was finished he still had one problem to overcome. One room of the new mansion was lined with bookshelves and the producer had not the slightest idea of what to put in those shelves. He did not want to risk displaying his own ignorance by attempting to purchase books himself. He had no idea of what "good" books he might buy to fill the empty spaces. Aside from the Bible and Shakespeare he could not think of a single book that would reflect his own good taste and erudition.

Among his employees, the producer knew of several who had reputations for being knowledgeable in literature. One of these, a young cameraman, he took aside. He quietly proposed to him that he take a week off, with pay, and spend the week purchasing books for the empty library. The only specifications the producer set were that the books must reflect good taste and knowledge in a wide variety of fields. He also asked that none of them be so modern that they might be controversial or offensive. He wouldn't mind, either, if they were all in fine bindings that would show his appreciation for the beauty as well as the content of the books, and reflect his ability to afford the best.

He gave the cameraman several signed blank checks, swore him to secrecy and sent him on his way.

The young man spent an enjoyable week. He purchased leather-bound editions of every literary classic he could find. He searched the bookstores of Los Angeles for rare and prized first editions. He gathered the finest art print books and rare, limited editions from European publishers. He checked his memory by going through university libraries. And he produced, in the end, a well-rounded collection of books representing the best thinkers in almost every area of human endeavor.

The producer was so pleased with the results that he gave the young man a bonus and once again impressed upon him the need for absolute silence.

Years later, the same cameraman happened to be discussing the work of the producer with a mutual acquaintance. The acquaintance remarked that he had recently attended a party at the producer's home.

"Oh? And did you happen to see his library?" the cameraman asked.

"I certainly did, he's very proud of it," the acquaintance said. He was smiling.

"Well, what did you think of it?" the cameraman asked.

"Well, it's pretty impressive. But you know, I started leafing through some books and the pages weren't even cut! When you start looking closely, none of it looks like it's been read. Some pretty old editions, too. But it sure does give the impression he's a scholar."

* * *

Most of Hollywood's film magnates were businessmen who saw an opportunity to make money in the industry. Few of them concerned themselves either with the artistic merits of their production or with the art of film making. They preferred instead to tend to the business of making profits.

In the early days of Hollywood film making, in fact, the business heads and producers would have had a hard time finding out about the various technical aspects of film production. Each man guarded his special knowledge and his special techniques as if they were gold. Special knowledge was money, for with no unions and with some producers anxious to get everyone in their family into the act, the man who had mastered one of the technical aspects of film making had a guaranteed meal ticket only so long as that mastery did not become common knowledge.

In those early days the cameraman operated his own camera, loaded and unloaded his film, personally took the exposed film to the processing laboratory and even took his own still photographs.

Abe and Julius Stern were producing a series of Baby Peggy comedies during the years just after World War I. The brothers were uneducated but shrewd and had made a fortune in the motion picture industry in only a few years' time. But their knowledge of the film making process was nonexistent.

Abe Stern kept a close eye on all the expenses for his operation and he observed one month that several hundred feet of raw film were missing. Stern was determined to find the thief.

Though the missing film cost relatively little and his own time might have been considered more valuable, Stern firmly believed that only by watching over every penny could he avoid ever-increasing extravagance and ever-decreasing profits. He decided to keep the matter quiet but to keep an eye personally on the entire crew of the Baby Peggy series.

Stern began to wander around the studio, checking locks, inspecting storerooms and unexpectedly dropping in at various offices.

He kept an especially close watch on Jerry Ash, the cameraman for the series, for Ash quite naturally had the readiest access to the studio film supply.

One day, during a lunch break, Stern noticed his cameraman leaving the stage with several cans of film. Stern followed him and got behind the stage just in time to see Ash disappear through a small doorway. When Ash returned to the stage, Stern took his pass key, hurriedly opened the door and switched on the light. He found himself in a small, windowless, closet-sized room. The room had little in it. There was no furniture and the single shelf across the far wall had stacked on it several film cans. Stern picked up one of the cans, ripped open a tape that sealed it and took out a full roll of film. He did the same with a second can and found that it, too, contained a full roll of the studio's film. He then opened a third and a fourth can.

At last he was satisfied that he had discovered the film thief. He angrily rushed onto the stage, brushed aside several actors who were going through a scene, and stood shaking his fist at the cameraman.

"What are you doing?" he blustered, half stuttering with rage. "You—a nice Jewish boy like you. A thief! A crook! Eating my bread, taking my money."

The normally good natured Ash finally interrupted his employer's diatribe. "What have I done?" he yelled.

"What have you done?" screamed Stern. "What have you done? How can you stand there and ask like that? You've robbed me blind. Because of you, I'm a poor man today." Stern grabbed Ash by the sleeve and started pulling him off the set toward the locked room, all the time muttering to himself in Yiddish.

Stern pulled out his pass key and unlocked the

little room. He threw the door open and snapped on the light.

"Look," he shouted, opening a can and pulling out the reel of film. In his excitement he let several dozen feet of film spill on the floor. "Look. And look here." He pulled open another can. "I found these all here this morning," he yelled. "And I opened them all and they *all* have film inside. What is this doing here? What do you think you are doing?"

Ash, completely dumfounded, looked sadly at the exposed film which he had shot that morning and unloaded at lunch time. He had intended to deliver it to the processing laboratory that evening, after finishing work.

"Mr. Stern," he pleaded, "this is the exposed film we shot this morning."

"Are you trying to kid me," Stern yelled. "You think I'm going to fall for that?" He scooped up some of the film that had unwound onto the floor and held it up in front of Ash. "You take me for a fool, young man? Me? I didn't get where I am being a fool! Look, look here, where are the pictures in your 'exposed film'?"

Ash whistled softly to himself and then tried, as gently as possible, to explain the photographic process to his boss.

Stern, still somewhat angry and not quite convinced, walked silently away. He retreated to his office, lit a big Havana cigar and began to compute the cost of the damage he had caused by interfering with the production when he could not grasp its technical aspects.

* * *

Abe Stern was not the only man in the film industry to face this particular embarrassment. During the early years, few people involved in the making of films were aware of the technical aspects of motion picture photography.

At Universal, in the early 1920s, Henry McRae was producing a silent film serial that concerned railways and railwaymen. At one point, the script called for a head-on collision between two locomotives. Since the scene was an important and costly one, the camera department sent along an extra assistant cameraman to help out. The young man had little experience in the film business.

The film crew set up two cameras so that the crash could be covered from different angles. The two old locomotives were positioned on a strip of abandoned railway track in the back lot of Universal's studio in the San Fernando Valley. When everything was prepared, the locomotives were started up with two stunt men at the controls. The men dived for safety just before the crash. The cameras had recorded a spectacular scene and the director was satisfied with his work.

The cameras were unloaded and the head cameraman gave the film magazine to the young assistant to be delivered to the darkroom. He took the magazines and walked off in the proper direction. Meanwhile, the rest of the camera crew began packing up their belongings and moving them to another part of the studio to continue shooting.

After fifteen minutes had gone by the head cameraman realized that he had forgotten to tell the young assistant that they would be moving. He sent another assistant back toward the studio buildings to look for him.

The assistant began his search at the darkroom. There he discovered that the young man had not been seen and had not deposited the film magazines. The assistant continued his search, each moment growing a little more panicky—not about the missing man, but about the important film magazines. He checked the still photography lab, hoping that the new man had simply found his way to the wrong darkroom. But the young cameraman had not been seen there either. Finally, after a half hour of searching, he walked back to the tracks where the crash scene had been filmed. And there, sitting near the railroad track, he found the new man busily attempting to shove the film back into a magazine.

"What are you doing?" the seasoned assistant demanded. He had real cause to feel panic by this time.

Conrad Veidt in Universal Studio silent production, *The Man Who Laughs,* 1928

The young man answered him with sincere puzzlement. "I just opened the magazine to see the crash, but I don't see anything on the film. What do you think could have happened?"

The old time cameraman stood beside the newcomer, scratching his head in disbelief. It was just too strange a situation to call for anger.

"Damn it," he said at last, "You'll really have hell to pay. You've ruined the shot. You've probably seen your last day around here."

But the newcomer was not fired. His uncle, it happened, was Carl Laemmle, the owner of Universal Studio. And the young man kept his job and went on to become one of the best known directors in Hollywood. His name was William Wyler.

Boris Karloff

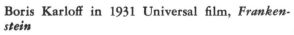

Boris Karloff in 1931 Universal film, *Franken-stein*

Makeup artist Jack Pierce at work creating original monster makeup for Frankenstein films. The model served to assure that makeup would be the same each time it was applied.

Dr. Frankenstein's laboratory

P.D.926

Boris Karloff and Mae Clark in *Frankenstein*

Another scene from same film

Boris Karloff

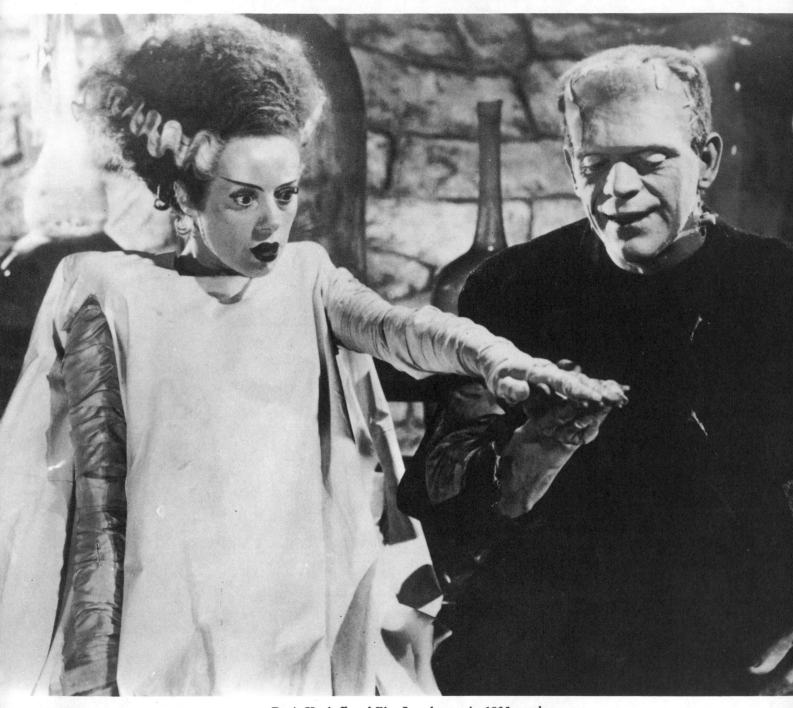

Boris Karloff and Elsa Lanchester in 1935 production, *Bride of Frankenstein*

Gloria Stuart and Eva Moore in 1932 Universal
film, *The Old Dark House*

Brember Wills and Melvyn Douglas in *The Old
Dark House*

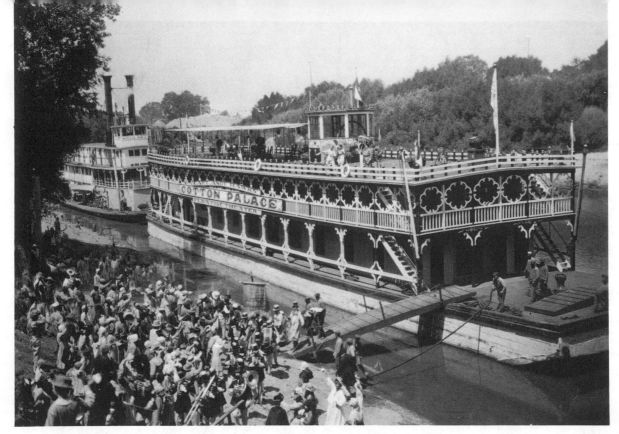

Showboat, 1929

Paul Robeson and Hattie McDaniels in Universal's 1936 *Showboat*

Allan Jones and Irene Dunne in *Showboat*

Charles Winninger as Captain Andy Hawks in 1936 *Showboat*

Universal director Edward Sloman illustrates a fine point for his actors on the set of 1927 silent film, *Surrender*

Scenes from Director Edward Sloman's film,
Foreign Legion, Universal, 1928

Cameraman Karl Freund (with cigar) and Director Scot Beal (seated in front) pose with other crew members on early version of crane designed to give camera crew more flexibility of camera angles

Scene from Academy Award winning production
of *All Quiet on the Western Front,* 1930. Lew
Ayres is standing in center

Scenes from *All Quiet on the Western Front.*
Film began as a silent production and was con-
verted to sound in the middle of shooting

Lew Ayres, second from right, in scene from *All Quiet on the Western Front*. The film was one of the most eloquent early anti-war statements made   45

Lew Ayres in Universal's *All Quiet on the Western Front*

Lew Ayres in Universal's *All Quiet on the Western Front*

Maurice Murphy and Barbara Reed in another
successful film based on World War I, *The Road
Back*

More scenes from 1937 production, *The Road
Back*

48

Larry Blake, Slim Summerville and Andy Devine
in *The Road Back*

Andy Devine in *The Road Back*

German Generals surrender to French in *The Road Back*

Mae Clark and Kent Douglas in 1931 production
Waterloo Bridge

Peggy Shannon and Allan Mowbray in 1935 film,
Night Life of the Gods

Peggy Shannon (second from left) and Allan
Mowbray in Universal's *Night Life of the Gods*

Edward Arnold in *Sutter's Gold*, 1936

Charles Wilson, Lee Tracy and Edward Arnold in
Sutter's Gold

Katherine Alexander and Edward Arnold, *Sutter's Gold*

Georges Renavent and "natives" face Charles
Bickford in 1931 production of *East of Borneo*

East of Borneo, Universal, 1931

Rose Hobart in *East of Borneo*

Diana Barrymore visits father John in his Hollywood mansion. Photos were taken when Diana first arrived in Hollywood during the late 1930s to pursue a film career. John Barrymore by this time was already past his prime as a leading man

Gloria Jean, Universal child star, reads book co-authored by Roman Freulich shortly after its release in 1939

Harold Adamson, George Murphy (former U.S. Senator from California and former film star) Ella Logan and Jimmy McHugh in *Top of the Town,* a 1937 Universal film

61

Mae West and W. C. Fields in *My Little Chicka-dee*, 1940

Joseph Calleia, Mae West and W. C. Fields in
My Little Chickadee

W. C. Fields gets his chance to play sheriff, *My
Little Chickadee*

2

"Carl Laemmle Presents..."

A glance at the history of motion pictures can make one curious about the men who were its first moguls. These men built the industry from a backyard operation with fixed camera and stage to something like a country within a country, with its own royalty, its own dictators and its own loyal subjects.

They were not men with training in the arts or in theater or literature. They came to the film industry by chance. They had seen opportunity where others had not. And, as often as not, they viewed the opportunity as they would view any other opportunity—as they would view the selling of shoes or of plumbing or of used cars. Profit was their motive. Any artistic achievement that may have come along the way was purely accidental.

One such man was Carl Laemmle.

Laemmle was born in the small town of Laupheim in Germany. He was a small man—only five feet tall—and unimposing. He might have seemed a genuine loser, for after coming to the United States in 1884 he spent ten years at odd jobs—sweeping floors, feeding pigs, running errands—without making any progress. It was only through the kindness of his wife's uncle that he was eventually given a job as a clothing salesman in Kenosha, Wisconsin.

Yet it was this unimposing little man who eventually purchased one and then two nickelodeon theaters and who went on from there to set up his own film distribution company. And it was this little man who broke the stranglehold of the General Film trust that had for years kept the industry static.

Laemmle may have appeared to be an unlikely candidate for flight from the law, yet at one point in his career he ran off to Cuba with a production company of his own creation and with Mary Pickford as star, while the lawyers and the lawmen followed in hot pursuit to attempt to prevent this upstart from cracking the tightly controlled film production business.

In 1912, Laemmle formed Universal Pictures Corporation along with several other men who had broken into the business during those early years. Before long he managed to take over complete control and in 1914, after several years of production in Hollywood, he moved his company to Universal City, the newly purchased headquarters in the San Fernando Valley.

Laemmle was not a young man when he began his career in the film industry. But in spite of his unremarkable earlier life, his was not a personality to be casually dealt with. Although he was generally considered to be a kindhearted man, he was still a no-nonsense executive who did not treat the spending of a dollar lightly. The new studio in the San Fernando Valley served to illustrate his thriftiness. From it he derived three incomes. The production of films, of course, was the major source of income. The second source was a chicken and egg farm which had been operating on the studio property when Laemmle purchased it. He saw to it that the chicken farm continued to operate—and at a profit. The third source was gambling—Laemmle allowed studio employees to gamble in the commissary and took a cut.

* * *

Laemmle himself loved to gamble and he was not willing to deny that pleasure to his employees, so long as he had a share in it. Gambling, in fact, was the subject of many stories told about Carl Laemmle. It was reported, for example, that several of Laemmle's employees managed to hold on to their jobs and even to wangle promotions to better paying jobs by gambling with Laemmle and losing just enough to be constantly in debt to him. He would then allow them to keep good positions in the studio so that they could continue to pay their gambling debts.

It was also reported that Laemmle liked to gamble in Mexico where the stakes were higher than most of his employees could afford. There, with professional gamblers, he could win or lose to his heart's content. But when he lost, all did not go well for his employees at Universal City. On one such occasion, Laemmle is said to have lost over $25,000. When he returned to Hollywood, he quickly ordered a cut in the salaries of the only studio employees who were not yet unionized—the clerical workers. Their salaries were raised again, but only after Laemmle had made up his gambling debts.

* * *

Laemmle's thriftiness came out in other ways. He often had to take business trips to the east coast and he looked forward to the long train rides that were involved. But he did not look forward to the dining car food nor the dining car prices. Although he was already a millionaire, the spending of a few dollars for poor food in a railway dining car went against his instincts. Good food, however, was quite another matter. So, before each trip to the east coast, Laemmle would send his secretary, Jack Ross, to the Jewish neighborhood of Los Angeles to stock up on kosher delicatessen items. The two would board the train with a huge hamper filled with corned beef and pastrami, smoked salmon, bagels and rye bread, coleslaw and dill pickles and tomatoes. The hamper would be given to the porter to be placed on ice. At mealtimes, the two men would sit in Laemmle's private compartment—another expense he did not object to—and eat their kosher picnic with cold beer or hot coffee purchased from the dining car. The drinks were the only items Laemmle would purchase on the train—enough, he felt, to warrant the special service of storing his delicatessen meals for him.

* * *

The thrift that Laemmle practiced in such odd ways was apparently passed on to other members of his family. His daughter, Rosabelle, considered herself a careful and thrifty shopper.

Rosabelle did love fashionable and expensive clothing. She would spend a good deal of her time throughout the year shopping at exclusive stores in Los Angeles and, once or twice a year, in New York. She enjoyed her clothing and she carefully saved the exclusive boxes with their exclusive labels.

When Christmas came, it was Rosabelle's job to purchase the gifts her father would distribute to various employees. Her purchase usually came from the bargain basements of the cheaper department stores of Los Angeles. But she would personally wrap each purchase in a box that was left over from her own shopping sprees.

* * *

Laemmle's interest in money went beyond merely saving what he had. He was always interested in new ways to make money. So single minded was he on the subject that people and events from other worlds than finance often completely escaped him.

At one time, the studio was visited by the famous German soprano, Lotte Lehmann. She and her husband were given red carpet treatment and when the studio general manager introduced them to Laemmle, he was so impressed that he decided to personally accompany them on their tour of the studio.

They were shown the stages, the offices, the various storage rooms for wardrobes and props, the laboratories where stills were developed, the back lots with their elaborate western and European village sets. They visited the chicken ranch and the Universal zoo, which by then had become quite famous. They were also taken to the commissary for lunch.

And all the while, between the explanations of the studio general manager, Laemmle kept asking questions. But his questions were not about opera and they were not addressed to his famous guest. In fact, he all but ignored the singer. His questions, instead, were addressed to her husband. They were about stocks and finance, about banking and business prospects.

The answers he got were, however, not very satisfactory. But he did not discover why until the couple was given a flowery introduction before the commissary luncheon. Laemmle, it seems,

had thought he was talking to the Lehman of the well-known New York banking institution.

* * *

Rosabelle Laemmle was the only daughter in the Laemmle family. Quite naturally, Carl Laemmle looked forward to her marriage and to having some grandchildren. He had always hoped that some of the young managers and directors he hired would take notice of her. But most of them had ideas that did not include marriage to the boss's daughter.

But at long last Rosabelle did find a young man. His name was Stanley Bergerman and he was, at the time, a floorwalker for the May Company department store in Los Angeles. The two fell in love and at long last Carl Laemmle was to have a son-in-law.

In celebration of the marriage, Laemmle recalled an old Jewish tradition that called for the doing of charitable deeds whenever one had happiness of his own to celebrate. The idea was to remember those less fortunate and to try to help them share a little in one's own happiness.

Laemmle, of course, looked upon the giving of charity as he looked upon everything else. There was no question that he would do what was necessary, but it would have to be done in such a way that his own pocketbook did not feel the pinch. At last he hit upon an idea. He called in the manager of his chicken farm and gave him instructions to send a truckload of chickens to the Jewish Home for the Aged in Boyle Heights, an East Los Angeles suburb.

The chickens were sent. The manager of the home thanked Laemmle profusely. And Laemmle was content that he had done all that was required—and done so with a generous spirit.

But the chickens had been cleverly picked out by the manager of the farm, so that there would be no slowdown in egg production. The manager had done his job well. He had picked out all the old hens—the ones that were no longer laying.

The chickens could not be broiled or roasted.

They were so old and so tough that they had to be boiled for hours before they could be eaten. For weeks the old people ate chicken soup and boiled chicken, chicken salad and chicken croquettes—chicken served in every way possible to disguise its tough and stringy quality.

But eventually the generosity of Laemmle became too much for the old people. For the first time in the history of the home, they went on a hunger strike. It was a successful one. The manager of the home took the remaining chickens and dumped them in an incinerator.

Meanwhile, the new son-in-law became an ex floorwalker. He took over his new tasks as general manager of Universal. And though some people claimed that the studio was being run like a department store, Bergerman did manage to keep most of the people working at Universal relatively happy.

* * *

Another of Carl Laemmle's habits—one that had much to do with his continuous interest in economizing—was to stroll onto sets at odd moments without sending word that he was coming.

His entry always brought terror to everyone on the set. In fact, so many people had been frightened by his visits that most directors got into the habit of stationing one crew member to look out for Laemmle and pass the word when he was coming.

There are, during any film production, many moments when a large number of people on the crew are idle. An electrician may be needed at a moment's notice, but he is not busy at every moment during the day. Extras may have to sit around for several hours, fully costumed and made up, before they are called onto the set. A hairdresser might be needed to straighten out a star's coiffure but might have nothing to do for long stretches of time. But the presence of all these people bothered the man who was paying for them and who had little understanding of the actual production of a film.

When word came that Uncle Carl (a name Laemmle himself encouraged the use of) was coming on the set, a frantic scene would quickly go into operation. People who had been sitting around reading papers, snoozing or playing cards would suddenly begin dashing back and forth, doing anything that might give them the appearance of being busy. Even directors who might otherwise have been working while sitting in their chairs felt obliged to get up and run around yelling orders.

On one such occasion, a young photographer took advantage of the director's need to run around to use his chair for a few moments' rest. And, as he should have been able to predict, Laemmle took one quick look around the set, saw a man sitting and headed straight for him.

"Why is it that everyone on this set is busy working and you are just sitting there, young man," Uncle Carl asked.

"You see, sir," the photographer replied, "the only time I ever sit down is when you come on the set. It's the only time I can find a chair."

* * *

Carl Laemmle, in spite of his penurious nature, was generous in one way. He loved his family and his native town of Laupheim and so it stood to reason that all who came from his family or from Laupheim should be able to find some kind of employment at Universal.

Carl Laemmle Jr. was, quite naturally, first in line. When he became old enough to want a job during the 1920s, he immediately became a producer at Universal. For awhile, directors managed to keep him busy without allowing him to interfere on the set. In fact, Carl Jr. became completely absorbed in his own special project. He hired an amateur basketball team and put the men to work as electricians and assistant directors. He even made one of the men his associate producer. On their off hours the men were expected to practice and Carl Jr. saw to it that they had plenty of off hours.

The basketball team took the championship of the California amateur league and went on to become national champions. The accomplishment was one Carl Laemmle Jr. was proud of—perhaps even prouder than of the films he was allowed to produce.

* * *

It was not unusual for a Universal film to be released with titles reading:
"Carl Laemmle Presents
A Carl Laemmle Jr. Production
Produced by Carl Laemmle Jr.
Directed by Edward Laemmle"
But the Laemmles were not the only family members to hold jobs at Universal.

Among the family nephews employed by Uncle Carl were several directors, Joe Levigard and William Wyler among them. Another nephew was employed as a casting director and quickly won a reputation for his lack of perception. He is said to have dismissed Bette Davis as being "cross eyed." He called Katherine Hepburn "consumptive" and turned her away. He refused to hire Rudolph Valentino because he was a "wop" and refused at first to hire Boris Karloff because he was a Russian. When it was explained to him that Karloff was in reality an Englishman named William Pratt, the casting director relented and Karloff went on to play in westerns until he received his first big break with the role of Frankenstein's monster.

* * *

Laemmle's generosity went beyond his relatives. He was equally magnanimous when it came to hiring people from his native Laupheim. Since Laemmle frequently contributed to various charities in Laupheim, word of the town's famous citizen spread and the flow of German immigrants to Laemmle's office was a constant one.

During the decade following World War I, Laemmle hired another casting director—an immigrant from his native village.

When casting was in progress for *All Quiet on the Western Front* in 1930, the studio decided that preference should be given to veterans for jobs as extras. Most of the extras were to play soldiers in the German army.

A group of veterans from the Hollywood post of the American Legion came to the studio to apply for jobs. Since the film was about German soldiers and since the casting director was still sympathetic toward his homeland, he quickly decided that he did not like these American veterans.

"What army did you serve in?" he asked the men.

"The American Army, of course," was the reply.

The casting director, knowing full well what the answer would be and knowing that eventually he would have to hire Americans for the film, could not restrain himself.

"Sorry," he told the veterans, "you won't do. You served in the wrong army." He then turned on his heels and walked out, leaving the veterans speechless. They had, after all, been informed that veterans were going to be given preference in getting the jobs. Just what kind of veterans did the studio mean?

It was a depression year and the men did not want to give up the jobs without a fight. They reported the incident to American Legion officials. And a very unpleasant situation might have developed for Universal. It was a difficult enough matter to bring out one of the first films that might be classified as anti-war. It was even more difficult to bring out a film that was sympathetic toward the German soldier of World War I. But to have the American Legion going to the press with a story that the studio had refused to hire American war veterans because they had fought in the wrong army would have been disastrous.

The studio had to put forth a mighty effort to cover up the event and to convince the American Legion that the film was not a pro-German film, but simply a film showing the horrors of war for all fighting men. The American veterans were hired, the event was successfully hushed up and

All Quiet on the Western Front became one of the film industry's all-time classics.

* * *

Among the Laupheimers given their first chance in the film industry by Uncle Carl was Kurt Newman. He came to Hollywood in the 1920s and went immediately to visit the man his father had once known in Laupheim. He was given a job as an apprentice in the editorial department and was assigned to work under a very competent film editor.

Newman was one of Laemmle's best Laupheim investments. He learned rapidly and earned his salary honestly. But that salary was for a long time too small for him to afford either elegant housing or a car. He lived in a rooming house in Hollywood and each day he got up early and stood on a corner by one of the main thoroughfares to San Fernando Valley to await a ride from a fellow employee.

But one morning, while he stood by the curb waiting for his ride, a truck swerved and Newman, instead of going to work, was brought to a hospital.

At the hospital Newman was asked for the name of his nearest relative. But he had no relatives in Los Angeles and had not been working at Universal long enough to have developed any close friendships. The only name he could think of was the name of his boss, Carl Laemmle.

As tight fisted as Laemmle was with his millions, he was still most generous when it came to the care of sick acquaintances. When he was informed of the accident he immediately gave the hospital instructions to give Newman a private room and to tend to all of his medical needs with speed and with the best possible doctors and supplies. Laemmle himself guaranteed that the bills would be paid.

Newman did get the best possible medical care but the amputation of one leg could not be prevented.

Eventually Newman was fitted with an artificial leg and returned to his job at the studio.

On his first day back he went into Laemmle's office to thank him for the care and attention he had received.

Newman was still new to the United States and to the cost of American medical care. He thanked Laemmle profusely for the fine care he had received and assured him that he intended to pay back every penny.

Uncle Carl was accustomed to being surrounded by people who were always happy to take from him and who rarely offered to give anything in return. He was so moved by the young man's naive and sincere pledge that he immediately began trying to figure out some way to help him achieve his goal. He knew Newman could never pay him back on the small salary he earned as an assistant film editor.

"Perhaps I can help you pay back the money," Laemmle said. And he did just that. Newman was moved out of the cutting room and given his own film production to direct. His salary, of course, was adjusted accordingly. And Newman proved to be one of the steadiest and most reliable directors Universal had.

* * *

But Laemmle was not always so lucky with the Laupheimers he hired. The story of another young Laupheimer was, unfortunately, not unique. The young man came to Hollywood during the silent film days. His first call, like so many other villagers, was to Uncle Carl.

Laemmle greeted the young man warmly, asked how things were in Laupheim and, meanwhile, observed the fact that the young man was tall and well built and would certainly be photogenic. After chatting in German for awhile, Laemmle asked the young man if he would like to become an actor. The Laupheimer did not have any particular job in mind when he came to Laemmle—but he did have *a* job in mind. Acting seemed better than he could have expected and he agreed to give it a try. Since there was no sound to worry about, he did not even have to worry about the inadequacy of his English.

Laemmle explained that he would have to begin as an extra and advised him to learn to ride a horse since his best chance for getting beyond the job of extra would probably come in one of the numerous two-reel westerns Universal made. The young man told Laemmle that he already knew how to ride a horse. Laemmle smiled with satisfaction. The tall, slim German would look fine in western dress.

Eventually the young man got his chance. His name was changed and for three years he rode the range and captured outlaws through a whole series of two reelers. But then talking pictures came and the acting career of the young Laupheimer was over.

But Uncle Carl never deserted his Laupheimers. While the careers of other, more famous, silent stars were completely cut off, Laemmle sent word to the young man. He would be welcome to continue working at Universal if he could see his way clear to taking the less prestigious job of sound technician. Since sound was new, the studio sound department was new. Since everyone was learning, it seemed a good time for the young man to also learn about the new techniques.

The young man did quite well in his new position and soon became a sound director. As the 1930s progressed he kept completely occupied with two main interests: the first was in every aspect of film making, the second was in the rise of the Nazi party in his homeland. The Laupheimer eventually joined the German American Bund. In his growing enthusiasm for the Nazi party, however, he became indiscreet. He began distributing literature quite openly at the studio and he solicited funds with a rather heavy hand among those who worked under him.

Word of his political activities soon got back to Laemmle. It was the one thing Uncle Carl could not tolerate. He had hired and promoted people simply because they were Laupheimers. Often he had passed over men of more talent out of friendship and fond memories of his native village. The rise of the Nazi party in Germany worried Laemmle, but there was little he could

do about that. However it seemed intolerable that in his own studio men should be allowed to spread vicious anti-semitic propaganda and extort funds from his employees.

The young Laupheimer was promptly fired. But he did not raise a protest. It was time, anyway, to return to his native land. He had funds by that time and skill in film making. He brought both to his new work of producing Nazi propaganda films in Germany.

* * *

Among the directors who worked at Universal who were not somehow related to Laemmle was James Whale, an Englishman who had begun his career in amateur theater. He, unlike some of the relatives and villagers, worked his way up from a job as a stagehand.

Whale was a taciturn and shy man. He relayed most of his orders through a burly Scotsman who worked as his assistant.

On one film he had long wanted to make, Whale had employed a number of English actors. Every afternoon at four he would call a halt to filming and sit down with these actors and with other British members of his crew for afternoon tea. The rest of the crew would wander outside the stage or play cards and chat until the filming continued. The habit persisted, despite signs of displeasure it brought from the studio management.

The general manager of Universal first witnessed the tea drinking when he happened by one day to talk to the production manager.

"How long has this been going on?" the general manager asked.

"Since filming started."

"And how long to drink a cup of tea?"

"About thirty minutes," was the reply.

The general manager sputtered with rage. "Do you realize that every cup of tea they drink is costing the studio about $200?" he asked. "Make them stop. You are the boss, not that tea drinking director!"

Perhaps if they had been filming a western the

production manager might have been able to get Whale to stop his four o'clock tea break. But they were not shooting a western, they were shooting a film based on an English Victorian novel.

The first film Whale directed at Universal was *Frankenstein.* The film was an enormous success. He next directed the film version of H. G. Wells's *The Invisible Man.* This film, too, was highly successful. But Whale had an enormous desire to direct films in his native England. To win sufficient reputation to accomplish that goal, he felt he should first direct a film worthy of British audiences rather than the less discriminating Americans. He picked a Victorian classic as his ticket to success in his homeland.

Whale and a cast of fine British actors labored over the production for several months. Certainly one could not fault the fine cast. At last the production was completed, the picture was edited and scored and released. But it was a disaster. Whale had forgotten that Victorian novels had long ceased to please both American and British audiences. In addition, Whale had made the mistake of tampering with the original novel sufficiently to displease even those few remaining addicts of Victorian novels.

Perhaps James Whale was ahead of his time. For the Victorian novel has found its audience once again in the age of television. The popular British series, *The Forsyte Saga,* based on John Galsworthy's novels of late Victorian life, has recently fascinated people who for years seemed interested in more violent viewing fare.

* * *

John Ford numbers among those who got their start during Laemmle's reign as chief of Universal. Ford attributes his start as a director to Laemmle's tight fisted reputation and to the terror he brought to everyone when he visited a set.

In a speech given recently at the University of California, Ford recalled that he had gone to Universal to work as an assistant property man on a set where his brother, Francis, was supposed to be directing a western. But Francis apparently did not show up. The studio general manager suddenly came rushing onto the set. He looked around, failed to spot the director and frantically called up the director's brother.

"Jack," he yelled, "do something. The boss is coming to watch us shoot this movie."

Ford recalls that he thought for a moment and then told all the cowboys on the set to come racing and screaming down the street of the western set. They did this just as Laemmle appeared to watch.

The general manager urged Ford on,

"Jack, do something else."

So Ford gathered the cowboys again.

"Now, next time, I'm going to fire a gun and I want a couple of you guys to fall off your horses."

He fired the gun and the men fell to the ground. And Laemmle again expressed satisfaction. But he did not leave.

Once again the general manager urged, "Do something, he's still here."

But the assistant property man was out of ideas.

"What can I do?" he asked.

"Anything, I don't care—set the town on fire."

So Ford called for some gasoline and burned down part of the set. And Laemmle was again satisfied.

A few weeks later a new western was about to go into production and when the general manager asked Laemmle who he wanted to direct it, he replied, "Check Jack Ford."

That, according to Ford, is the way he got started as a film director.

* * *

Not every Universal director satisfied Laemmle as easily as did John Ford. The penurious Laemmle was bound to clash openly and often with the perfectionist nature of Erich Von Stroheim.

"A tree is a tree, a rock is a rock; shoot it in Griffith Park." That statement is often said to be characteristic of the old-time movie managers who were interested only in the profits their films could make. The philosophy expressed in that statement and the philosophy of Erich Von Stroheim were poles apart.

Von Stroheim was an absolutist when it came to realism. He would accept no substitutes. And the bill for the real thing often became immense. Among his famous films were *Blind Husbands, The Devil's Passkey, Foolish Wives, Merry Go Round, Greed, The Merry Widow* and *Queen Kelly.* And on all of them he insisted on his own brand of realism, down to the smallest detail.

A tree, to Von Stroheim, was not just a tree. It was always a very particular tree. And it would not do if it was not *the* particular tree called for in the script. He once stopped production for a full day because six birch trees called for in one scene turned up as fabricated jobs, straight from the studio property shop. Real trees—birch trees of the proper shape and size—had to be located, purchased, and trucked to the set while the crew waited.

On another film, the studio paid thousands of dollars to have medals designed and made up for a mythical country. Von Stroheim would not settle on something from a Los Angeles pawn shop, though the medals never appeared in such close shots that their faces could be read.

Once he is said to have insisted that a complete and workable phone system be installed in a multi-room hotel set. The phones were never used.

Real food and real liquor were always used on Von Stroheim sets, even when no one ate or drank. And if the shooting had to be done several times, the food and liquor were replaced lest they appear cold or flat.

On one production Von Stroheim ordered that all the stars be fitted with silk underwear so that they would feel properly aristocratic in their roles as royalty. It did not matter to Von Stroheim that the blue-blooded underwear was never seen.

His realism eventually proved too costly for the studio. But Von Stroheim's contributions to the progress of the industry were undoubtedly larger than the bills he ran up at Universal.

* * *

The financial success stories at Universal were not the artistic successes. Von Stroheim, for all his genius and his reputation, did not turn out the kind of moneymakers that kept Universal in profits.

One such box-office success occurred when some one at Universal got the idea of combining the talents of Mae West and W. C. Fields in one film.

The negotiations were not simple. Miss West agreed to the film, but with the provision that Fields abstain from drinking during working hours. Eventually Fields agreed to the restriction: it was simple enough to carry around a soft drink glass all day, and he denied that there was ever anything else in it.

Miss West became so enthusiastic about the project that she helped to write the script for the film, which was titled *My Little Chickadee.*

The filming was touchy from the beginning. Fields never managed to arrive on the set on time. He refused to rehearse until he had inspected all the cameras to convince himself that none of them were loaded. And when his quarrels with the director became too strident, he would retreat to the front porch of his dressing room where he sat in his rocking chair and drank his "Coke" and rocked himself back into good humor while the crew waited.

As is often the case with talented comedians, both Miss West and Fields threatened to ruin the film with their attempts to upstage one another. The crew added to the mayhem by their enthusiastic appreciation of the two stars and their antics. But director Ed Cline saved the film by tactfully shooting an enormous amount of closeup footage. Each of the stars was able to shine without the fear of audiences being distracted by the other.

* * *

Probably the biggest financial success Universal produced during the 1930s was the work of two Hungarians. Joe Pasternak and Henry Koster had been film makers in Hungary and both had come to the United States in the mid-1930s when the rise of Nazism in Germany seemed to them to threaten the future of all Europe. Both found jobs at Universal and together they were assigned a moderate-budget picture. Pasternak was to produce the film and Koster to direct.

When the script was finished the two began casting. Since the depression had slowed production all over Hollywood, they were able to hire Charles Winninger and Alice Brady for their film, in spite of their modest budget. The film was called *Three Smart Girls,* and for their three girls Koster and Pasternak wanted Barbara Reed, Nan Gray and Jane Withers. The first two actresses were hired, but before the third could be signed, the studio general manager asked Koster and Pasternak to use a young actress the studio already had under contract. Koster insisted that the film needed someone who already had an established reputation. The general manager insisted that there were enough such actors in the film, that the acting budget had already gotten too high, and that there was no reason for them to look outside the studio when they had a perfectly acceptable young actress right there. Koster again objected, as the young actress was inexperienced and not an outstanding beauty. She even had a slightly deformed arm that was the result of a childhood accident. The general manager finally ordered Koster to use the girl. She was already under contract to the studio at $75 a week and she did have a good singing voice. At this point Koster was ready to quit. The cost of hiring another good and established actress did not bother him. This was to be his first Hollywood film and he had no desire to have it spoiled by a newcomer.

But Pasternak convinced his friend to stay on and the film went into production. Koster tried to achieve perfection. But the studio had seen enough of the techniques used by Von Stroheim. This was going to be a budget film if the general manager had to stand over Koster every day.

And the general manager did nag. He often stood on the sidelines and called out when Koster tried too often to do extra takes on a single scene.

"Hey, you!" he would yell, "that scene looked okay to me. You think you're making some kind of blockbuster?"

In spite of all the tugging and hauling, *Three Smart Girls* did turn out to be a kind of blockbuster. The film, which cost the studio no more than the average B picture, proved to be a smash hit at the box office upon its release and cleared millions of dollars for the studio.

And Deanna Durbin, the young actress Koster had fought so hard to avoid using, became an overnight star. She went on to make one musical hit after another. Her name was used to endorse all kinds of products and Deanna Durbin dolls became the popular forerunner of Shirley Temple dolls in the hearts of little girls all over the United States.

* * *

The success of the Durbin films brought many American notables to Universal. Among them was Jerome Kern, who wrote a musical for a Durbin film.

While the film was in production, Kern would often come to the studio to watch and to listen to the recording of the sound track and background score. He was asked at one point how he came to write film scores so quickly and easily. Kern, who had little respect for the movies, replied, "Every composer has a trunk full of stuff which isn't good enough. When the studio asked me to do this score, I just went through my trunk, polished up a few things and gave the studio the score."

* * *

Not every starlet who came to Universal was as successful as Deanna Durbin, and the stories of some of these girls are not ones to make the film industry proud. During the 1930s, Universal, while still not willing to break any of the long-held traditions concerning the roles it was proper for a Black woman to fill on film, nevertheless signed a contract with a young Black whose beautiful figure, fine features and dusky complexion made her natural star material.

Since the studio was unwilling to buck what they felt would be a negative reaction on the part of the public to a Black star, the publicity department was put to work to think of some way to use the girl without revealing her background. She was dark, but not too dark to permit some deception.

The publicists quickly came up with a scheme. They would present her to the public with every bit of the fanfare ordinarily accorded to a new starlet. And they would present her as an East Indian princess.

The wardrobe department designed an exotic costume for her and the publicity department created a new name to go with the new image. Though the name certainly could not fool anyone with a knowledge of Indian culture, the publicity department found it appropriate. They called her Burnu Acquanetta.

Studio photographers did a whole series of sittings with the young woman. Publicists wrote dozens of releases announcing the talents of the new star. And photographers and releases were soon sent to newspapers and magazines all over the world. She was hailed as the greatest discovery since Greta Garbo and the story of her royal background was played for all it was worth.

Several studio producers, anxious to take quick advantage of the work done by the publicity department, vied with one another to have Acquanetta appear in their productions. And in a few short months a film with Acquanetta in an important role was ready to be released.

But at about the same time the studio was suddenly faced with a major crisis. The wide publicity given to their new find had backfired. From a small town in Ohio a small group of upright citizens had begun a letter writing campaign. These indignant Americans threatened to expose the studio and see to it that the whole

world came to know that Universal was trying to hoodwink its customers by passing off a Negro girl from Ohio as an Indian princess.

The studio management somehow mollified the irate Ohioans. But Acquanetta was never again given the opportunity to appear in a featured role.

Since she was still under contract, however, something had to be done with her. And a place was found for her by one of Universal's producers —a man who specialized in horror films. In her first role for him her body was displayed to advantage—covered only by a few well-placed animal skins. But since she had to play the role of a monster, her face was made up to look like the face of an ape.

* * *

Diana Barrymore came to Universal during the 1930s with the reputation of her famous family behind her. Her father, John, had already made several films at Universal, but he was well beyond the peak of his career. His famous face was puffy from alcoholism and his great profile no longer had the fine outline that had once captured so many women.

But John Barrymore made the effort to greet his daughter when her train arrived in Los Angeles. It was a true Hollywood reception, attended mostly by photographers and newspapermen. Diana stepped out to greet her father, and after posing for photographs with him went to a hotel. Her mother, long-divorced from John, had prevailed upon her to live away from the supposedly evil influences of her father.

She did, however, pose with her father at his home. The home was bare, except for a few stiff pieces of furniture and a suit of armor that stood in one corner of the huge living room. And John Barrymore managed to keep his daughter amused and smiling through the whole sitting, for John had a seemingly unending repertoire of dirty jokes.

But in spite of the bravado, the sitting was undoubtedly difficult for John Barrymore. He had seen little of his daughter during her growing years and now that he had her with him for awhile, he could not communicate his feelings. When the sitting was over and Diana was preparing to return to her hotel, Barrymore's face sagged and he fought back tears.

Diana, who had been signed on the basis of her famous name, was a star before she made a single film. The process of making that first film was a painful one. Diana could satisfy no one: the make up men found fault with her face, the wardrobe department complained that she was impossible to dress attractively and the director did not like the way she delivered her lines. Her Hollywood sojourn was neither long nor successful, and the career of the girl with the famous name ended with her suicide.

Her brother, John Drew Barrymore, also attempted a movie career, but it was even shorter and less impressive than Diana's. The Barrymore talent and the Barrymore looks were unfortunately not commodities that could be passed on to a second generation.

* * *

The stars who passed through Universal and the directors who made films there did not greatly impress Carl Laemmle. Even Barrymore was just another name to Uncle Carl. He had created too many actors and directors out of relatives and friends to be impressed or overawed by what these people did.

The techniques of film making and acting were to his mind not difficult to master. But quite typically, Laemmle did value the story of his own success. He knew how hard won *that* was for he had gone through it. He had not become an overnight director or actor—these people he created with a word or two. He had arrived at his own position by a much more difficult road and at a much later time in life than had most of the famous people he created.

When Uncle Carl reached his sixtieth birthday in 1929, he was flattered, but not completely surprised, when his employees decided he deserved a great celebration to honor his accomplishments.

This, of course, was not the end of his career and many of the stories we have told about him and about Universal occurred after this celebration. But it seems fitting to close this chapter with this particular story because it is so typical of Laemmle and of his career. For while many of his employees went out of their way to belittle him, Carl Laemmle's ego remained undamaged. He was a man who, above all else, knew the value of what he had accomplished.

A great banquet was planned for Uncle Carl's sixtieth birthday. All the employees of the studio were invited and a number of executives from other studios were asked to join in the celebration. The food was excellent and plentiful and it was accompanied by the best wines and, of course, good German beer. As the meal drew to a close, the speeches and entertainment began. Studio actresses sang or did dramatic readings. Actors clowned. Executives gave laudatory speeches.

Everyone, it seemed, owed what they were to Carl Laemmle and he was extolled as a man who could take his place beside Washington, Jefferson and Lincoln on the American scene. And Laemmle did not see anything superfluous or embarrassing about the praise that was heaped upon him.

The following day, one of his Laupheim friends—a studio executive who had come to Laemmle without funds or talent directly from his native village—came into Uncle Carl's office still ablaze with enthusiasm.

"You know," he said, leaning back in his chair and patting his stomach with contentment, "even I hadn't realized . . . even I . . . how much you've accomplished. It's really something. You should tell the world about it. You should write a book."

Laemmle waved the idea aside modestly, but his mind started churning it over. At last he replied.

"I can't do it. I don't have the time. And I'm no writer."

"That's nothing. You just hire someone to do

it. You really should. What an inspiration to American youth!"

"You really think so?" Laemmle asked.

"Not just me," his friend insisted. "Everyone around here would love to see you do it!" The man was somewhat carried away by his own enthusiasm.

"But who could do it?" Laemmle asked, now getting really interested.

"Well, what about this English writer who just did the play on Lincoln. Name's John Drinkwater, I think."

"Lincoln? He did a play about Lincoln? Does he work for us?"

"No," the friend explained, "he lives in England. But he could probably be hired."

"Well," mused Laemmle, "if he could do Lincoln, I suppose he could do me."

So the studio executive got to work. He wired Drinkwater and, after several more wires, sent him a contract and a ticket to Hollywood.

Drinkwater received a large advance and set himself up in a comfortable apartment in Hollywood and then he began his work. The biography was eventually completed and it proved to be a very long and detailed one. It was published in two weighty volumes and received rather indifferent notices from weary reviewers who bogged down in the first few chapters.

But at the Universal Studios Commissary a huge display of the biography appeared alongside the cigars, candy and newspapers at the cashiers counter. For weeks the volumes sold as quickly as they could be uncrated. And for even more weeks Laemmle went around the studio with a look of great satisfaction as he eyed all of his employees going about with carefully dog-eared copies of his biography under their arms.

Maria Montez

Maria Montez

Lou Costello and Bud Abbott, Universal comedy
team

Universal Studio executives, left to right: Jules Bernheim, Stanley Bergerman, Dale Van Every, Richard Schayer, Carl Laemmle Jr., Carl Laemmle, E. M. Asher and Felix Young

Douglas Fairbanks Jr. and Danielle Darrieux in
Rage of Paris, 1938

From *Rage of Paris,* Mischa Auer, Danielle Darrieux, Douglas Fairbanks, Jr.

Universal actresses Peggy Moran, Constance
Moore and Ann Nagel

Louise Albritton

Peggy Moran

Peggy Moran

Burnu Acquanetta

Grace McDonald

Grace McDonald and Charles Winninger

June Vincent

June Vincent

Turhan Bey

Susanna Foster

Susanna Foster

Elyse Knox

Anne Gwynne

Diana Barrymore

Donald O'Connor says goodnight to his mother
in studio publicity shot

Jane Withers

Chariot chase scene, *The Boys From Syracuse*

Comedian Joe Penner in scene from 1940 film,
The Boys From Syracuse

95

Martha Raye in Universal's *The Boys From Syracuse*

Allan Jones and Irene Hervey in *The Boys From Syracuse*

Barbara Reed and Ray Milland in 1937 film,
Three Smart Girls

Kay Francis and Walter Pidgeon in Universal
film, *It's a Date,* 1940

Carole Lombard and William Powell in 1936
production, *My Man, Godfrey*

Universal's *My Man, Godfrey,* Eugene Pallette,
Carole Lombard, Alice Brady and Mischa Auer

Gail Patrick and Carole Lombard in *My Man,
Godfrey*

Loretta Young

Loretta Young

Loretta Young

Deanna Durbin in her first film, *Three Smart Girls,* produced at Universal in 1937

Barbara Reed, Deanna Durbin, Nan Grey,
Charles Winninger and Binnie Barnes in
Three Smart Girls

Deanna Durbin, Nan Grey and Helen Parrish
in 1939 production, *Three Smart Girls Grow Up*

Eugene Pallette, Adolphe Menjou and Deanna
Durbin in *One Hundred Men and a Girl*, 1937

S. Z. Sakall, Deanna Durbin and Robert Cummings in Universal's 1940 film, *Spring Parade*

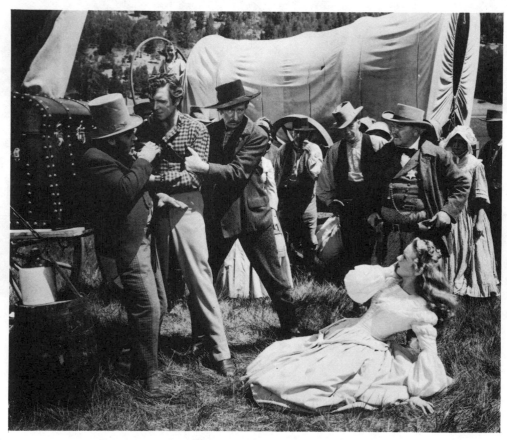

Akim Tamiroff, Robert Paige, George Cleveland and Deanna Durbin in 1944 release, *Can't Help Singing*

Deanna Durbin with six of her leading men:

Jackie Cooper (*That Certain Age*, 1938)

Lewis Howard (*It's a Date*, 1940)

Robert Stack (*Nice Girl?*, 1941)

Edmond O'Brien (*The Amazing Mrs. Holiday,*
1943)

Joseph Cotten (*Hers to Hold*, 1943)

Gene Kelly (*Christmas Holiday*, 1944)

Deanna Durbin

Deanna Durbin

3

"Put some money on Republic"

Mack Sennett invested heavily in Mexican oil in the early days of the film industry. When the Mexican government nationalized the industry, Sennett was left with nothing but his studio. That he had to sell to a man named Nat Levine. The Mack Sennett Studio in San Fernando Valley became the Mascot Studio.

It was from Levine that Herbert J. Yates purchased the studio. He renamed it Republic Studio and it rapidly became famous for its corner on the western film market.

The numerous Roy Rogers, Wild Bill Elliot, Gene Autry and John Wayne films that were cranked out under the Republic label often obscured the fact that the studio did, in fact, produce something other than horse operas. During those years when the cowboy was king at Republic, stars named Ethel Barrymore, Myrna Loy, Robert Mitchum, Charles Laughton, James Mason and Orson Welles were also making films at Republic—and not all of them were westerns.

But is was all the same to Herbert J. Yates. He, like Laemmle at an earlier date at Universal, was interested in a healthy balance sheet. The fact that his studio was considered the horse opera center of the film industry did not matter in the least. He was neither proud of it nor embarrassed

by it. He was first and foremost a businessman.

Since Yates was not one of the early studio owners, he is seldom mentioned in the histories of Hollywood. He was nonetheless a colorful character. The dour Scotsman was in his own way as tight fisted as was Carl Laemmle.

When he took over the old Sennett studio in the days before the Second World War, he had hardly noticed the green trees and the flowers and little patches of lawn that bordered the walkways of the studio. Republic was then one of the nicest looking studios in Hollywood.

But no matter how long he ran the studio, Yates was constantly searching for ways to save money. And one day, as he walked around his domain, it suddenly occurred to him that he had passed several gardeners—all of them busily trimming grass or cultivating flower beds. He returned to his office and called in the studio accountant.

"How many gardeners do we have?" he asked.

After making a few phone calls the accountant assured him that there were no more than ten—six who worked at gardening full time and four who spent part of their time tending to other maintenance chores.

"How much do we pay them?" Yates asked.

The information was supplied and the decision was simple for Yates to make. Although the total payroll of the gardeners amounted to far less than the pay of one of his class B western stars, Yates ordered that all of the gardeners be put to work killing the grass and flowers and uprooting the trees. When the job was done the men were either transferred to other work or fired.

Asphalt was installed where the flower and grass borders had once been, and what had been one of the most beautiful studios in Hollywood became the studio with the lowest maintenance cost.

* * *

With economy as his motive, Yates would often spend part of his days lecturing to directors, producers and production managers who had allowed their productions to slip behind schedule. Usually his lectures would be followed by promises that the production crew would try harder and would make up the time.

But Herbert J. Yates met his match when he made that familiar complaint to director John Ford. Ford was not a man to allow bullying from the front office to interfere with his method of operating.

On one production, Ford had allowed the schedule to slip a few days. And true to form, Yates discovered the misdemeanor and came to the set to talk to Ford. He waited patiently for a break in the shooting—he did not want to slow things down even more. Then he approached Ford.

"You realize, Mr. Ford, that you're four days behind schedule," Yates said.

Ford looked down at Yates, then calmly picked up the script. Without looking at it he tore out a page. He flipped a few pages and tore out a second page, then a third and then a fourth. Then he calmly told Yates: "Don't worry, son, we're right on schedule."

* * *

There were few things about Republic Studio that could be considered extravagances. But Yates did indulge one habit that called for a strange bit of extravagance here and there. The studio was well equipped with what had become an obsolete item in most places. Every office and every stage and every laboratory where Yates might possibly set foot was equipped with a cuspidor for the boss. And these were kept carefully cleaned and ready. No one would dare throw an old tissue or a Coke botttle in a cuspidor. They were for the exclusive use of the boss—the one man in all the western film making territory who still chewed tobacco.

* * *

Although he was not above cutting the number of people on his payroll, Herbert J. Yates was not a man to underpay his employees. Those who remained on the payroll received good wages for their work. Unlike Carl Laemmle, Yates did not give his employees dimestore Christmas gifts wrapped in exclusive boxes. Each year his people received huge baskets crammed full with gourmet foods and fine Scotch whiskey.

Like Laemmle, Yates was a gambler. And like Laemmle, he maintained a rather indulgent view of gambling on the studio grounds and on studio time.

There was a good deal of gambling around Republic, as there was at most other studios. It was especially common during the years of World War II. Film making had been classified as an essential industry—the endless numbers of uniformed boy meets defense-worker girl movies that were turned out during those years were somehow considered essential to America's fighting morale.

But before the essential classification had been given the industry, film makers had feared that they would have to shut down because of a loss of personnel through the military draft. Shortly after the war started, the studios scrambled to hire extra help and most of them continued to maintain double crews through the war years.

While few men were drafted from the industry during the war, a large number did volunteer for service, so the policy might have been partially justified. Certainly the film industry was one of the few industries in the United States that did not suffer from a labor shortage during those years.

But the many extra men had idle hours to spend and so gambling increased during the war years. And Yates tolerated it gladly since the extra help served as his insurance against incomplete crews.

In his morning strolls around the studio Yates frequently came across groups of men playing poker or shooting craps. On one such stroll he stopped to watch the gamblers. After a few moments, one of them turned around and commented.

"Mr. Yates, we're playing with your money. And I've got most of it."

Yates wiped a bit of chewing tobacco from his lips and laughed.

"You call that gambling? When I gamble I do it for millions." He snorted, laughed once again and walked off the stage, leaving the men, who often risked their entire salary, feeling as though they had been caught playing a children's game.

But unlike Carl Laemmle, Yates never took out his own gambling losses by temporarily reducing the salaries of his own employees.

* * *

Yates, however, was not above trying to take money from his employees by outwitting them.

He came one morning to the gallery of his chief photographer and greeted him cheerfully. He took off the Sherlock Holmes cap that was his traditional headgear and then looked around for his cuspidor. After getting rid of his wad of tobacco he made himself comfortable and called the photographer, who had only recently been hired by Yates, and in a conspiratorial voice asked him if he would like to make some money.

The photographer shrugged his shoulders.

"I'm not letting many people in on this and I'll expect you to keep it quiet," Yates continued. "Put some money on Republic stock. It's selling

for seven and an eighth now. Big things are coming. I know! You'll make a bundle. Put everything you've got on it." Yates then told a few old army jokes, shuffled his feet a bit and got up to leave.

A few minutes later a camera director came into the gallery.

"Was that the old man in here?" he asked.

"Yes, he just left," the photographer answered.

"I bet he gave you a hot tip on Republic stock."

"How did you know?" asked the surprised photographer.

"Listen," said the cinematographer, "the old man has tried that on everyone—he's tried to bilk everyone in this studio. He's selling the stock now. Then he'll drive the price down. And when guys like you have to get out to save what's left of your shirts, then he'll buy back—at maybe three, three and a half. Forget about it. Forget about trying to play in his league. He's a real pro. You know, I just snoop around and see when he's selling. When he sells, I sell. I just sold 1000 shares this morning. I bought them for five and three quarters. I'll buy back when Yates is ready to buy."

* * *

Yates's attempts to manipulate stocks at the expense of his employees were common knowledge to everyone who had been at Republic for long, but he apparently thought the secret was well guarded. At any rate, he considered himself worthy of the respect of one and all. And since he did not stint when it came to salaries, he did, in fact, have the respect of his employees. While they laughed at his sharp dealings they did not bear any grudges against him for them.

Except for the economy with the gardeners, Yates rarely fired anyone without good reason. Only once did he allow personal pique to color his judgment.

The regular daytime gatekeeper at Republic had held his job for a number of years and had always greeted Yates with a warm smile and a courteous, "Good Morning." He had even removed his cap each time the big boss came by in his chauffeur-driven limousine.

The gatekeeper was rarely ill. But one morning he called in and said he would be unable to come to work. His substitute was another of the studio security guards—a man who rarely saw the people from the executive offices. He was instructed to stop all cars coming in and check to be sure the occupants really had business in the studio. The procedure was an old one which had, in fact, been instituted by Yates himself.

When Yates and his chauffeur appeared at the gate, the guard stopped them.

"Who are you?" the guard asked.

"Why, this is Mr. Yates," the chauffeur replied.

"Who's he?" the guard asked.

The chauffeur explained that Yates was president of the studio and only then did the guard let him pass. But Yates was already furious. The idea that one of his employees did not even know his name or recognize his face was incomprehensible to him and the fact that the man had not even removed his cap added to his rage. No sooner did Yates get seated behind his own desk than he asked his secretary to phone the studio security chief and find out who the man was. The security guard was fired.

* * *

Yates's inability to take personal disrespect was the cause of some rather difficult moments for his employees. He was, however, rather insensitive and he rarely took anything short of a direct affront as a sign of disrespect.

On one occasion he even failed to notice that a large group of his employees was laughing directly at him. This occurred at the conclusion of shooting on a film called *Timberjack.*

Yates had gone on location himself and was throwing a big banquet for the entire crew. He was a meat and potatoes man and so the food at the banquet was plain but plentiful and of excellent quality. The crew members were served fine steaks with plenty of salad and potatoes and enough Scotch whiskey to wash everything down.

After the banquet, Yates himself got up to give a speech. He was normally a taciturn man and yet he felt obliged on this occasion to entertain his employees. He began his speech with a few short sentences of praise for each of the stars and each of the crew members and by the time he had worked his way down to the property men and the grips everyone was getting a little drunk and a little sleepy. At last he was ready to conclude his talk. And he decided to conclude it with a joke.

The joke has passed into oblivion. Few people who attended that banquet could remember it, even the next morning. But Yates thought it was mightily funny. He, in fact, laughed so hard that he dropped his teeth. The whole crew then started laughing uproariously.

When Yates managed to get his teeth back in place he looked up with a grin of satisfaction, waved to everyone and left the room. He was convinced that the crew had been laughing at his joke and he was content with that.

* * *

Timberjack had been a particularly important film to Yates because it starred the woman he had taken special interest in.

Vera Hruba had come to the United States from her home in Czechoslovakia to compete in her specialty, which was ice skating. She then became interested in a film career, but nothing much came of it until she caught the eye of Herbert J. Yates.

She had never displayed much acting talent and she was not an outstanding beauty. And she was no longer particularly young. But she did win the love of the aging owner of Republic and she suddenly became the leading lady of the studio.

Vera Hruba became Vera Ralston and soon she and her mother were living at Yates's San Fernando Valley mansion. But her father was a man of the old world and of old world morality and he frowned upon the arrangement.

Hruba had been a jewelry merchant in Czechoslovakia before the war and when the Communists took over he managed to find a job as a minor government official. His wife and daughter had come to the United States before the war in hopes of furthering Vera's ice skating career. Through the war years it had been impossible for them to get together. But several years after the Communist takeover, Hruba managed to make a trip to the United States. He was not very enthusiastic about what he found. His notion of a successful career for his daughter had little to do with starring in second rate films or living with a man older than he was.

Hruba's stay in the United States was a short one. Unable to convince his daughter or his wife to return to Czechoslovakia with him, he nevertheless decided that life under a Communist regime was preferable to staying in the United States and watching them pursue fame through the film industry. He remained just long enough to have some teeth extracted and have a dental plate made. Then, equipped with his new dentures, he returned to his homeland and refused even to correspond with his wife or his daughter.

In spite of backing by Yates, Vera Ralston never became a true star. Everything possible was done for her but she was never able to overcome the limitations of her own small talent and beauty. Today there are few film fans who even recall her name.

* * *

But there were others who were discovered at Republic who did not share that fate. The story of Roy Rogers is one of true Hollywood success.

Certainly Rogers never was one of Hollywood's dramatic greats. But he did combine the wholesome looks and the easy going singing style that made him one of the best-known and most successful stars of the singing cowboy films of the 1940s and 1950s. He came along at just the right moment in the history of films. Probably no one would buy his kind of talent today, although

his television guest appearances still please his old film followers.

The young cowboy singer had come to Hollywood to be discovered. Since Republic was already the western film making center, Rogers placed himself outside the main gate at that studio. Every day, as Yates passed through, Rogers would be there happily strumming his guitar and singing a western song.

From that modest beginning, Rogers became one of Republic's biggest stars. Yates simply brought him in, had screen tests made and began starring him in western films.

The combination of Rogers with Trigger, the educated horse, and later with Dale Evans, assured him a long and lucrative career in the singing western. And Rogers was content to stay in that role—a role he filled successfully for a number of years.

The famous Trigger, the horse who could count and perform so many other intelligent feats, was in reality four horses. Each of these carefully picked carbon copies was trained to do one or two different tricks. The combined effort produced the superhorse of film fame.

* * *

John Wayne was another regular at Republic. After a good many attempts at other types of roles during his first years in films, Wayne found his niche in the two-fisted western, playing either good bad guys or maverick good guys.

But, unlike Rogers, Wayne never stayed exclusively with the western. His long and popular career was always spiced with films of other types —films such as *The Quiet Man,* which he made at Republic under the direction of his long-time friend, John Ford. And, during and after World War II, Wayne also starred in a series of war films such as *The Sands of Iwo Jima.* It was these films that gave him a second image as a tough U.S. fighting man.

Still, the image most Americans carry of Wayne is of the Western hero—tough, slightly ornery, but basically gold inside. That image, strangely enough, is the one that even those people who worked closely with Wayne carry with them.

Even before he began to openly show his political colors, Wayne had a reputation in Hollywood among those who knew him as a political reactionary. Yet, on the set, he has always been one of the most generous and easy going stars to work with. It seems that his political feelings about the working man were something abstract and removed from his feelings about the working men who helped make his films.

* * *

Orson Welles was the opposite of Wayne. While he openly preached liberal politics he had the reputation of being a most difficult man to work with. One reason for this reputation was his own creative drive. He was, and undoubtedly still is, a man of great creative energy and has always been in a great hurry to complete his projects and get on to the next ones.

When working on *Macbeth,* which he produced and directed at Republic, Welles drove the entire cast and crew at top speed. The film was completed in four weeks. So it seemed, at first, that the on-stage tyranny had paid off.

Welles had shot the film with a fine cast of actors: Welles himself had played Macbeth. Jeanette Nolan had played Lady Macbeth, and Dan O'Herlihy, Edgar Barrier, Alan Napier and Keen Curtis were also in the cast.

But the complete production had been done in an old Scots dialect. It was impossible to understand and could not be exhibited in the United States until it was dubbed.

While the production had set new records in time saved, the dubbing took months to complete. And when it was finally released, the film was universally panned by critics as dull and heavy-handed.

John Ford

John Wayne in 1949 Republic Production, *Sands of Iwo Jima*

John Wayne, *Sands of Iwo Jima*

John Wayne

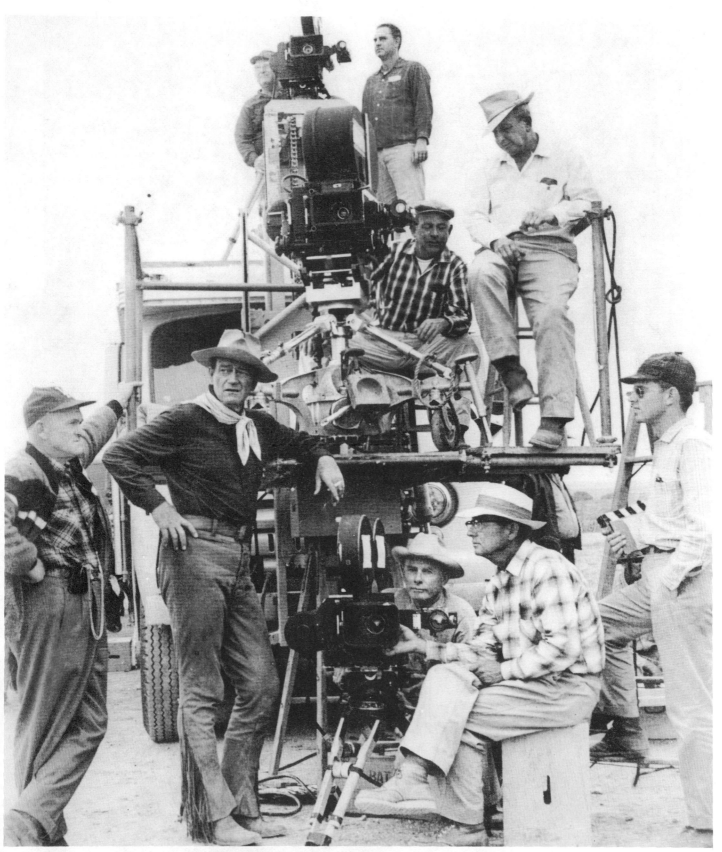

John Wayne and crew of United Artists' *The Alamo*

John Wayne (far left) on set of *The Alamo,* 1960

John Wayne

Estalita Rodrigues

Chill Wills

Chill Wills

Joseph Schildkraut in costume for 1946 film,
The Plainsman and the Lady

Ilona Massey

127

128   Ilona Massey

Ethel Barrymore

Ivan Kirov and Viola Essen in Ben Hecht production of *Spectre of the Rose,* filmed at Republic in 1946

Ivan Kirov and Viola Essen, *Spectre of the Rose*

Judy Canova

Eddie Foy Jr. and Judy Canova

Composer Aaron Copeland

Aaron Copeland conducting score he wrote for Republic's 1949 production of *The Red Pony*

Bill Elliot

James Mason

Louis Calhern

June Havoc and James Mason

Ken Murray in 1947 Republic production, *Bill and Coo*

136

Herbert J. Yates, head of Republic Studios during the 1940s and 1950s

Dale Evans

Gloria Swanson

Andy Devine

Jane Frazee

Joan Crawford and Scott Brady in 1954 Republic production, *Johnny Guitar*

Joan Crawford and John Carradine, *Johnny Guitar*

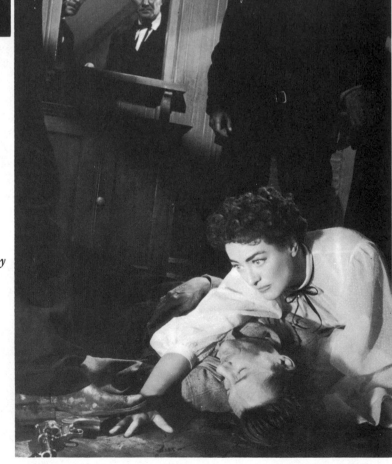

142

Joan Crawford, *Johnny Guitar*

Jane Russell

Jane Russell

Vera Ralston

Vera Ralston

Vera Ralston

148

Adele Mara in Academy Award winning pinup
pose

Orson Welles in Republic's *Macbeth*, 1948

Erskine Sanford in *Macbeth*

John Dierkes in *Macbeth*

John Dierkes in another role in *Macbeth*

Peggy Webber, *Macbeth*

Ken Curtis, *Macbeth*

4

"Someone is click clicking away"

When production on any film begins, the problems begin. Whether they be with actors or extras or photographers or publicity men, every film that has been made has had problems. And every film has had its accompanying stories of difficulties and delays.

Actors themselves may be the problems. Particularly when they must sort out their own feelings upon being required to do difficult scenes.

In the early 1960s, a remake of *The Cabinet of Dr. Caligari* was produced. In it Glynis Johns was required to do a striptease. The sound stage was hushed. Miss Johns was slowly removing her clothing. The cameras whirred.

But in the middle of the scene, Miss Johns stopped abruptly, turned and pointed to the still photographer.

"Get that man out of here," she yelled.

The director rushed out to deal with his unruly star.

"Get him out of here," she kept repeating. "I don't want any indecent pictures made of me."

And so the still photographer was banished from the stage for the remainder of the scene. And Glynis Johns went on stripping in front of the motion picture cameras—without giving the matter another thought.

* * *

The casting of extras has often been a problem for film directors.

During the depression years, clever directors who wanted cheap footage of a mob would simply move their actors or stunt men to a main street in Venice, a beachside Los Angeles suburb where the unemployed frequently came to spend their idle days. The director would stage a fight, send idle crew members out to run through the street yelling, "Fight, fight," and shoot the results. Whether the crowd came to watch or to join in the melee made little difference. The film footage was useful. Scenes could be changed to match the event or the footage could be put aside for future use.

But when costumed extras were needed the process could not be so simple or so inexpensive. Sometimes people actually had to be hired to make up a costumed mob. And the difficulties such situations caused could not always be blamed upon potential extras.

One of the most persistent problems was finding extras for those persistent westerns. Indians, especially, have always been hard to come by—and the shortage seems natural enough when one examines the roles available for most Indians in American westerns.

But even when Indians have been available they have not always lived up to the producers' unrealistic expectations for them.

One astute production manager, on location in Washington State, hired 100 Apaches. He had high hopes of saving the film company a great deal of money since the Indians had agreed to live in tents and cook their own food on location. The savings in hotel and restaurant bills would be significant.

The film moved along on schedule until the director assembled the Apaches one morning at the edge of a river and asked them to get into canoes and paddle through some rather dangerous looking rapids. The Apaches, as the production manager should have known, had never learned to use canoes.

The director's tantrum, the production manager's threats of suicide, the grumbling of the entire crew did nothing to move the adamant Indians. The actors and crew members finally went back to their hotels to play poker. The Apaches returned to their tents. And the production manager and director had a nervous conference.

There was only one way to save the situation. A quick call was made to the studio in Hollywood and several dozen stunt men were rounded up. The men arrived at the location site the next day. They were given Indian costumes and wigs, their faces and bodies were stained, and they were set to work paddling the canoes through the rapids. The Apaches lined the river banks, avidly watching the phony Indians at work.

* * *

When *How the West was Won* was made a similar problem developed. The film called for a group of Indians to herd buffalo. But men who had experience in herding buffalo were rare in Hollywood. Once again, a group of Hollywood stunt men were sent for and disguised as Indians and the filming went ahead without incident—but at far higher salaries than the studio would have had to pay for extras.

* * *

On another western, this one a quickie, low-budget production, twenty Indians were needed. Since the film was being made in the Simi Valley just outside of Los Angeles, there were no problems related to the expense of housing or feeding extras. But the production manager, familiar with the going rate for Hollywood Indians, told the producer that the cost would be $10 plus a box lunch per day per Indian.

The producer, who had a long line of quickie successes behind him, was an expert at cutting corners. He brushed aside the production manager's figures.

"Go downtown to the L.A. plaza and pick out twenty husky looking Mexicans," he said. "I know you can get them for $5 a day—they'll even bring their own lunch. We'll fix up the script while you're gone."

So the film was made, with a few lines rewritten. The Indians of the original script had become a band of halfbreeds.

* * *

During the 1920s and 1930s—and for some photographers on into the present time—the 8 by 10 camera was considered the mainstay of the still photographer while shooting photos on the set. But one enterprising young photographer at Universal had been experimenting with the use of 35 millimeter cameras.

During the shooting of *One Hundred Men and a Girl,* the photographer decided to put his knowledge of the small camera to work. He took his Leica on the set and began shooting stills. To avoid any suspicion that he might be loafing, he also carried his 8 by 10 camera onto the set.

One Hundred Men and a Girl starred Deanna Durbin, Mischa Auer, Adolphe Menjou and Alice Brady. It also starred symphony conductor Leopold Stokowski—a man who was very fussy about conditions when he was working on the set.

The photographer worked quietly with his 35 millimeter camera for a few days without being noticed. The results were so successful that he began carelessly leaving his 8 by 10 camera on the sidelines, well out of easy reach.

One scene in the film depicted a concert. The film set was transformed into a symphony stage and 100 musicians were brought in to be filmed playing a Tchaikovsky symphony with Leopold Stokowski conducting.

The photographer left his 8 by 10 camera behind, found himself a good vantage point and began taking pictures with his Leica.

Suddenly Stokowski tapped his baton and called a halt to the music. He flourished his baton at the director.

"There is someone in here who is click clicking away with a camera," he announced loudly. In spite of the sounds of a 100-man orchestra he had heard that small foreign noise. He looked around, spotted the still photographer, and demanded that he leave the set.

The photographer waved a friendly greeting to the maestro, packed up his camera and walked off the set. He went to the studio processing laboratory and asked if his 35 millimeter film could be developed at once.

When the film was developed, he selected a half dozen of the best shots and asked the laboratory technician to enlarge them. A few hours later he was back on the set waiting for a break in the shooting. When a break came he followed Stokowski to his dressing room and greeted him in Polish, hoping to break the ice with their shared national background.

Stokowski smiled. Apparently it was not the first time someone had tried to speak to him in Polish.

"I'm not Polish," he explained. "My name is really Stokes. But you know American audiences are always more impressed by foreign sounding names."

The photographer, though he had not been able to communicate in Polish, had, at least, broken the ice. He took out the enlargements he had just had made and showed them to the conductor.

Stokowski was so impressed that he invited the photographer to return to the set and to continue "clicking away" as much as he wished.

But the troubles with the Leica were not over for the photographer. No one in the film industry considered the 35 millimeter camera a professional piece of equipment. In fact, the small camera did not become popular with photographers until well after the Second World War.

But the photographer was so pleased with his small camera that he did continue "clicking away." Eventually someone was bound to catch up with him.

One day the studio general manager visited the set of *One Hundred Men and a Girl.* He saw a man dashing about with a tiny camera and concluded that somehow a tourist had gotten loose within the studio and was making the most of it with his amateur camera. He called the studio's chief of police and told him, "Clear that rubberneck out of here." The photographer was cleared out without any opportunity to explain. He had no choice but to go home, although it was not yet noon.

A few hours later, the head of the photographic department called to ask the photographer why he had walked off the set. The photographer explained the situation and was back on the set the next morning.

And the 35 millimeter shots of Stokowski were entered in an international exhibition of Leica photography, where they received several top awards.

* * *

Economy minded producers have also caused

problems for property men—those men who supply and often design or create the props that are necessary for every film sequence.

As the film industry developed, the creation of fake properties became an amazingly complex art. Rocks made of *papier mâché* and trees made of plaster were easier to move and far more convenient than the real thing.

One of Hollywood's early masters at creating properties was Bob Lazlo. Lazlo was the first person in Hollywood to manufacture furniture and railings of balsa wood that could be used in fight scenes. The barroom brawl with its flying furniture would have been impossible without the easily shattered props, as injury to the actors would have made such fight scenes too hazardous.

Lazlo was also the first property man in Hollywood to use catsup for blood and the first to use Pancho Villa Mexican money when the United States government prohibited taking pictures of American currency.

At Universal during the silent days, Lazlo worked on a film called *The Invisible Man*. One scene in the film required that a pair of trousers float across the screen as if a man were walking in them.

After trying out and discarding several ideas, Lazlo purchased $50 worth of wire and sent the bill to the studio production manager. The production manager, being of the tight fisted school, called Lazlo into his office and demanded an explanation.

"What could anyone possibly do with so much wire?" he asked.

"It's for the trick photography," Lazlo explained.

"What do you mean?" the production manager insisted.

Lazlo tried to explain that the wire had been necessary to operate the trousers in their march across the stage.

"This is just nonsense," the production manager said. "What do you think you're trying to pull? I saw the rushes of those scenes. I didn't see any wire."

Lazlo decided that there was little he could do to convince the production manager. He got up and left the office.

But the production manager did not want to drop the matter. Once control of costs was lost, he felt, there was no telling what kinds of expenses would show up on his desk. He went to the set and called aside the film's director, James Whale, and asked him about the wire.

This time he accepted the explanation, which was almost identical to Lazlo's. And for the remainder of the filming, he stayed clear of the set and avoided the now amused property master.

* * *

Lazlo was one of the cleverest men in Hollywood when it came to inventing props on the spot. His quick thinking often saved valuable production time.

In the 1920s, Edward Sloman made a silent film titled *Foreign Legion*. Part of the film was shot in a desert area just north of Santa Barbara, California. In one scene, the script called for a violent sandstorm. A line of soldiers was to struggle through the sand, along with a wagon drawn by two mules. The sandstorm was to upset the wagon, killing the two mules. Then the legionnaires were to stop to bury the mules.

The director could not, of course, attempt to bury two live and struggling mules. Nor could he have the mules killed for the sake of the script. Instead, Lazlo, who was the property master for the film, brought in two *papier mâché* mules that had been made in his shop at Universal.

But at the last minute Sloman noticed that the paper mules lacked ears. The whole crew could have waited a day while the property man returned to his shop to make up a couple of sets of ears. But instead Lazlo took a pair of leggings from one of the extras who was dressed as a legionnaire. He cut the leggings and folded them into four ears.

An interesting sidelight: It was on the shooting of *Foreign Legion* that a dolly was used for the first time in Hollywood. The primitive contraption allowed the camera to be rolled back and forth on tracks so that it was possible to get moving shots.

* * *

Location often provides film people with the opportunity to meet people who are not accessible to most of us. During the filming of *The Hoodlum Priest* in the early 1960s, for example, the crew spent some time inside the Missouri State Prison at Jefferson City. Neither the prison facilities nor the prisoners were particularly pleasant. The buildings were gray and dirty. They had the massive and foreboding ugliness one often associates with the idea of prison. And very few of the men were allowed to go to and from their work unguarded. The contact that the crew had with the prisoners was mostly limited to inmates yelling obscenities through the bars as the crew passed.

But now and then a trustee would strike up a conversation with a crew member. One such prisoner happened one morning to pass by the still photographer, who was sitting on a stairway reading the morning paper. The photographer had placed three cameras by his side and the trustee eyed them with great curiosity.

A few moments later the photographer noticed the same man passing by once again.

The trustee passed by a third time, then doubled back and stood in front of the photographer.

"Mister," he said at last, "you with that film bunch?"

"Yes, I am," the photographer replied.

"What you need so many cameras for?" the trustee asked.

The photographer explained the different uses of his cameras.

The trustee listened patiently and then asked: "What's that one worth?" He had pointed to a Speed Graphlex.

The photographer told him that he had paid $300 for the camera.

"Well, I'll be damned," said the trustee. He let out a long whistle. "Last time I stole one of them things the pawnbroker gave me a lousy twenty-five bucks for it. Guess I was gypped!"

* * *

Gypped he was—and he was on the inside paying for his crimes. But often the film crew on location could count on encountering the gyppers —who, like the pawnbroker, were still on the outside enjoying their prosperity.

The art of fleecing the film folk is old and honored in popular location towns. And where new locations are found the local folk have quite often been quick to learn. Prices suddenly rise and services become scarce so that they become more valuable.

The Night of the Iguana was shot at Puerto Vallarta, Mexico. An American socialite welcomed the stars and the top men of the crew by throwing a party in their honor. Two dozen members of the film company were greeted by her at the town's finest nightclub. The hostess had arranged a lavish evening. She insisted again and again that her guests have more drinks and more food.

At last the evening came to an end. The hostess, who had arranged matters beforehand with her escort, sent that gentleman out so that the bill could be paid inconspicuously. The gentleman settled the account in the kitchen and returned to escort his socialite friend to her home.

Several of the film people had already drifted back to their hotels, but some had lingered on at the nightclub. As they prepared to leave, another bill was presented to a well-dressed member of the cast. He assumed that their hostess, who had never left the table, had forgotten to pay. Since he did not wish to be involved in an embarrassing scene, he, too, paid the bill.

The people of Puerto Vallarta had learned.

* * *

For the Black actor location could be particularly trying. While he often had to face humiliating real estate restrictions in California, he could at least make a life for himself where he could escape the constant reminders of his segregated society. Between home and studio Southern California could be relatively mild and untroubled by his presence. As long as he earned enough to dress well and drive a nice car he did not have to face the daily problems his poorer brothers faced. But no such escape was possible on location—especially on location in the South.

Rex Ingram is no stranger to the difficulties of being black and being an actor. A fine actor with experience on Broadway as well as in films, Ingram was often forced to accept minor parts that did not allow him to display his great talent. The reason was simple. Until recently there were absolutely no leading parts written for Blacks. The idea would have given nightmares to studio executives, who were thoroughly convinced that movies simply could not sell with Blacks in anything other than minor roles. While most of these men were sincerely liberal and sincerely concerned with social problems, they harbored all the fears of their fellow businessmen in other industries and continued to prefer the safety of what had been done in the past to innovation.

And so, actors of the caliber of Rex Ingram often found themselves accepting minor roles.

On a film called *Desire in the Dust* Ingram accepted just such a role.

The crew moved to Baton Rouge, Louisiana, for part of the filming. The entire Hollywood production staff was housed in a modern motel that featured a large swimming pool and a good restaurant. But Ingram was forced to stay across the city in accommodations that were open to Blacks.

Since much of the filming was done in the countryside, the company arranged with a local catering organization to furnish meals when they were needed during working hours. The food was served cafeteria style, with the crew lining up to be served. Since many of the grips and electricians were men who were hired locally, Ingram was careful to line up with the Hollywood part of the crew. The locals, he well knew,

would not make things pleasant for him should he try to join them.

But the major problems Ingram encountered centered around his accommodations. In order to get to the location site on time he had to leave his hotel before its small restaurant was open. Since he could not eat at the hotel where the rest of the crew was accommodated, he had to wait until lunchtime to eat his first meal.

Transportation to and from his hotel became another problem. A number of local teamsters were hired by the production company to transport the workers back and forth to location. Early in the filming one of these locals refused to take Ingram to his hotel, claiming it was against his principles to act as a chauffeur for a "nigger." The production manager, who was from Hollywood, did not let the incident pass. The teamster was told he would either chauffeur Ingram or leave the job.

The man quickly backed down. His job, it seems, was more important than his "principles." The experience did illustrate that there were some in Hollywood who would not put up with the folk customs of those afflicted with racism. But though it may have eased the pain a little, certainly it did not obliterate it for Ingram.

* * *

Publicity requires a very special kind of gift. In the heyday of Hollywood it called for much more than a vivid imagination and the ability to fabricate fiction that could pass as fact. The good publicity man was equally expert in turning truth to good advantage.

The filming of *Barabbas,* for example, had been timed to take advantage of a solar eclipse that would duplicate the eclipse that supposedly had taken place during the actual crucifixion of Barabbas. The film producers had found a small town near Rome where the countryside was to be used as background for the scene and where weather was fairly sure to be favorable for the filming.

It was simple enough for the publicity man to round up photographers and reporters from the European press. And his own men and the film's still photographers did the rest. Shortly after the eclipse the newspapers of the world were saturated with shots of the spectacular scene. Of course, each story mentioned that shots had been taken on the set of the movie *Barabbas*.

* * *

Simply taking advantage of nature is not always possible. Publicity is often harder to come by. So, with great regularity, the publicity man is forced to depend upon his own wit and inventiveness.

While the filming of Leo Tolstoy's *Resurrection* was in progress, a clever publicist named Harry Wilson read that Queen Marie of Rumania was to visit Hollywood. He quickly devised a scheme to take advantage of the royal visit. He had the film's producer, Edward Carew, draw a certified check for $25,000 made out to Queen Marie. The check was then offered to the Queen in exchange for one day of work on the film.

The offer was naturally made in public, with a number of newsmen and photographers looking on. The Queen was not present. But she was forced to reply. And, as expected, she rejected the offer. But the publicity gained probably added considerably to the gross revenue the film produced.

* * *

A similar device was used to publicize the filming of a Bob Hope film called *I'll Take Sweden*. The publicity man one day released the story that President Johnson's daughter Lynda Byrd was going to make her film debut in that movie. No offer had been made to Lynda Byrd and, if it had,

it would probably have been turned down. But the desired publicity was obtained.

* * *

When things become too quiet on location, a good publicity man often feels he must do something to earn his keep or the film he is supposed to remind the public of will fall into oblivion. And this is exactly what happened on a United Artists film on location in Acapulco, Mexico.

The publicity man and the still photographer got together to try to dream up something to bring the film production up out of the obscurity into which they felt it had fallen. Eventually they hit upon a scheme.

The next day they asked the film's star, Richard Widmark, to put aside time for a special series of publicity photos. Widmark obliged without asking what the photos were for. He merely assumed they would be used as standard handouts to newspapers and magazines.

The following day the publicist and the photographer went to Mexico City to visit the various news services. At each stop they left a few undeveloped negatives and a story which the publicist had written up. A day later the world learned that Richard Widmark, while on location near Acapulco, had saved the terrified natives of a small village from the ravages of a huge python snake. The snake, according to the story, had been terrifying everybody and had even killed one infant. Widmark, the story went on, had singlehandedly gone out to hunt the snake and had shot it, saving the innocent villagers.

Most Hollywood actors would take such a story in stride. They know that well over one half of the publicity put out while films are in production is false—and they merely assume that no one else could possibly believe it. Therefore, they might conclude, no one is hurt by it and the name of the film and of the stars is kept before the public.

But Widmark did not see things that way. When he saw the story in the English-language newspaper from Mexico City, he became furious and insisted that the overly active publicist and still photographer be fired.

The men were given their paychecks and plane tickets to Los Angeles and were sent in a company car to Mexico City. Once there they discovered that there would be a three-day wait because of tourist bookings. The two men had no objection to waiting. They were put up, at company expense, in a fine hotel. And they had plenty of free time to visit Mexico City's tourist attractions.

After a day of exploring, the two men encountered a fellow American in the lobby of their hotel. The man was a producer the publicist had once worked for. He had read the Widmark story and liked it. He was, he said, in Mexico to make preliminary arrangements for a film he would soon begin shooting. He had his star with him and wondered if he might not take advantage of the publicist and photographer to get a little publicity from the chance meeting.

He offered the men $500 each if they could dream up some story to plant in the papers.

Once again the two put their heads together and once again they came up with an idea. They went to a handicraft bazaar and picked up the biggest basket they could find—it had to be large enough for the star, Linda Crystal, to fit into. They then collected a huge bundle of Mexican paper money. Miss Crystal was placed in the basket, covered with the Mexican bills, and photographed with only her bare legs and bare arms and shoulders and head exposed.

The photographs were then planted with the wire services along with a story about Linda Crystal, the million dollar baby. The story claimed that the star had been insured by the producer for a million dollars for the duration of film production.

Photographs of pretty girls always seem to find room in newspapers. And the story and photograph soon made their way to dozens of front pages all over the United States.

The delighted producer had gotten his share

of the kind of publicity that had been scorned by Widmark.

* * *

On another picture—this one for Walter Wanger on location in Lone Pine, California—the same publicist and photographer used slightly more devious methods and came up with another scheme to make the newspapers.

The film was an Arabian nights fantasy that called for the usual scantily clad harem.

The town of Lone Pine offered little opportunity for spectacular stories. But this did not stop the team. The photographer took a number of pictures of the harem girls and then the publicist was ready to go to work. He went to the town sheriff, presented him with a bottle of bourbon and a $50 bill and convinced him to establish a 9 P.M. curfew for the girls. The sheriff agreed to release a statement that the curfew was for the girls' protection. Since there were so many girls around, it just wasn't safe for them to be out after dark. His department was too small to protect them all.

When the girls learned of the "curfew" they called a strike—at the publicity man's insistence. He had created a newsworthy situation and as long as the preparation for it was kept quiet, it would work.

Los Angeles papers began calling in and asking for pictures of the girls and for a few days the film's producer received all the publicity he could possibly want.

* * *

Publicity men are often employed to build the reputation of some newcomer rather than to gain attention for a film in production. Sometimes it is the studio that pays the publicist, but at others it is the aspiring star.

One young starlet who was under contract to Universal and felt that she was getting nowhere hired a publicity man to boost her career.

He simply had the starlet parade up and down in front of the studio gate. Every half hour the young lady would remove one item of her clothing. Word was sent out to the local papers and photographers began to gather. The starlet stripped to her bra and panties—certainly not very spectacular today, but an event in the 1930s. Photographs appeared in newspapers all over the United States and Universal executives had little choice. They gave the young lady more roles and a larger salary. The time was right to capitalize on the publicity the girl had gotten for herself.

* * *

Another publicist, faced with a similar situation, created a fashion institute at his office. He then took his charge to some of the best stores in Los Angeles, bought her some elegant outfits—all on approval—and had dozens of photographs of her made. His fashion institute then awarded the girl the title of best dressed Hollywood starlet. The photos were distributed to magazines and newspapers all over the United States. The wardrobe was returned to the stores. And the girl got a starring role in a minor film.

* * *

Human stars and starlets are not the only ones to receive the personal attention of publicists. Animal stars have always been valuable—sometimes even more valuable than the human stars who act with them. So Roy Rogers's horse Trigger—or rather horses—were given a buildup for intelligence. And Francis, the talking mule star from Universal, had to have some special image built up for him. He could hardly be praised because of his fine voice—no one would actually believe that it wasn't dubbed. Instead, a Universal publicity man talked the Los Angeles

Humane Society into granting an annual award called a "Patsy." It would be the animal equivalent of the Academy award. And Francis was the first to receive it.

* * *

Sometimes publicists would merely make news for their own delight—or to convince themselves that they could, in fact, do so.

During the late 1930s, a Los Angeles columnist and a studio publicist happened one day to be eating together at a Jewish restaurant in downtown Los Angeles. Among the people in the restaurant they happened to notice a man who bore a striking resemblance to Albert Einstein. They approached the man and began talking with him.

He had often been mistaken for Einstein, he said, and he rather enjoyed the joke.

The opportunity was too good to pass up. The two men offered to take the Einstein double out that evening and he agreed. They spent a busy afternoon. First they hired a chauffeur and the limousine that had belonged to Rudolph Valentino. They they rounded up invitations to a premiere that was to take place that night at Grauman's Chinese Theater. Next they rented tuxedos for themselves and their new friend.

When evening came they picked up their make believe Einstein and timed their arrival at the theater at the height of the crowd. As soon as the carbon copy Einstein stepped out he was surrounded by admiring mobs. Sid Grauman himself rushed out to greet the man and spent several minutes telling him how he admired his great work.

After the premiere the three men went to a plush restaurant for an elaborate supper. They never bothered to tell Grauman or anyone else that their Einstein was a fake. They had proved to themselves that they could create a good story —and that was enough.

Glynis Johns in 20th Century Fox 1962 remake
of *Cabinet of Caligari*

Glynis Johns in *Cabinet of Caligari*

Dan O'Herlihy plays Dr. Caligari

Dan O'Herlihy as greatly aged Dr. Caligari

Extras in East Indian costume pass the time between calls by playing cards

Extra waits for filming

Two extras take a break

Extras in western film chat while waiting for
their call

More card playing by waiting extras

"Settler" and "Indian" wait peacefully together,
possibly for a scene in which the "Indians" attack
wagon train

169

Blind harpist waits for his call

Leopold Stokowski conducts orchestra on set of
One Hundred Men and a Girl, 1937

Stokowski, *One Hundred Men and a Girl*

Leopold Stokowski

173

Leopold Stokowski in prize winning 35 mm photograph

Crew members pull first film dolly, rubber wheeled cart pulled along wooden track to give camera more flexibility, on set of 1928 film, *Foreign Legion*

Cavalry charge . . .

Rex Ingram

And Indian defense

A typical western shootout

More typical scenes from typical western films

184

Robert Ryan and Jack Lord in 1958 United
Artists production of *God's Little Acre*

Aldo Ray and Tina Louise in *God's Little Acre*

Tina Louise waits in bathtub while crew pre-
pares to film scene for *God's Little Acre*

Susan Hayward in United Artists 1958 film, *I Want to Live*

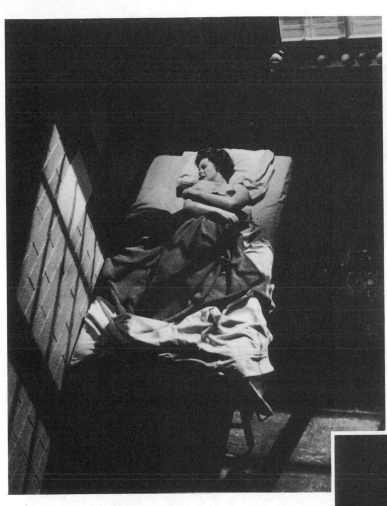

Susan Hayward, *I Want to Live*

Theodore Bikel and Susan Hayward, *I Want to Live*

189

Susan Hayward, *I Want to Live*

Jack Webb

Jack Webb in *The D. I.*

Ben Alexander and Jack Webb in scene from popular TV series, *Dragnet*

193

Frank Sinatra and Keenan Wynn in *A Hole in
the Head*, 1959

Frank Sinatra and chorus girls, *A Hole in the
Head*

194

Frank Sinatra on Florida shore, *A Hole in the Head*

Virna Lisi in 1965 United Artists production,
How to Murder Your Wife

Virna Lisi and Jack Lemmon, *How to Murder Your Wife*

Index

Abbott, Bud, 78
Academy Award, 12, 42, 149
Acquanetta, Burnu, 74, 84
Adamson, Harold, 61
Alamo, The, 123, 124
Albritton, Louise, 82
Alexander, Ben, 193
Alexander, Katherine, 56
All Quiet on the Western Front, 42, 43, 44, 45, 46, 47, 68, 69
Amazing Mrs. Holiday, The, 110
American Legion, 68
Apaches, 156
Arnold, Edward, 55, 56
Ash, Jerry, 23, 24
Asher, E. M., 79
Auer, Mischa, 81, 100, 157
Autry, Gene, 114
Ayers, Lew, 42, 45, 46, 47

Baby Peggy, 15, 23
Barabbas, 160, 161
Barnes, Binnie, 104
Barrier, Edgar, 119
Barrymore, Diana, 59, 60, 74, 75, 93
Barrymore, Ethel, 114, 129
Barrymore, John, 59, 60, 74, 75
Barrymore, John Drew, 75
Beal, Scot, 41
Bergerman, Stanley, 66, 67, 79
Bernheim, Jules, 79
Bey, Turhan, 88
Bickford, Charles, 57
Bikel, Theodore, 189
Bill and Coo, 136
Blacks, 12, 73, 159, 160
Blake, Larry, 51
Blind Husbands, 72
Boys from Syracuse, The, 95, 96, 97
Brady, Alice, 100, 157
Brady, Scott, 142
Bride of Frankenstein, 30
Broken Earth, 12

Cabinet of Dr. Caligari, The, 155, 164, 165, 166
Calhern, Louis, 134
Calleia, Joseph, 63
Canova, Judy, 131
Can't Help Singing, 106
Carew, Edward, 161
Carradine, John, 142
Christmas Holiday, 111
Clark, Mae, 29, 53
Cleveland, George, 106
Cline, Ed, 72
Cohn, Harry, 20, 21
Columbia Studios, 20
Cooper, Jackie, 107
Copeland, Aaron, 132, 133
Costello, Lou, 78
Cotton, Joseph, 111
Crane, 41
Crawford, Joan, 142, 143
Crystal, Linda, 162
Cummings, Robert, 106
Curtis, Ken, 119, 154

Darrieux, Danielle, 80, 81
Davies, Marion, 21
Davis, Bette, 68
DeMille, Cecil B., 21
Desire in the Dust, 160
Devil's Passkey, The, 72
Devine, Andy, 51, 141
D.I., The, 103
Dierkes, John, 152, 153
Dolly, 174, 175
Douglas, Kent, 53
Douglas, Melvyn, 31
Dragnet, 193
Drinkwater, John, 76
Dunne, Irene, 33, 35
Durbin, Deanna, 73, 103–113, 157

East of Borneo, 57, 58
Einstein, Albert, 163

Elliot, Wild Bill, 114, 133
Essen, Viola, 130, 131
Evans, Dale, 118, 139
Extras, 155, 156, 167, 168, 169

Fairbanks, Douglas Jr., 80, 81
Fields, W. C., 62, 63, 72
Foolish Wives, 72
Ford, Francis, 71
Ford, John, 71, 115, 118, 119
Foreign Legion, 37–40, 158, 174, 175
Forsyte Saga, The, 71
Foster, Susanna, 89
Foy, Eddie Jr., 131
Francis (the talking mule), 163
Francis, Kay, 98
Frankenstein, 26–29, 68, 71
Frazee, Jane, 140
Freulich, Roman, 11, 12, 61, 137
Freund, Karl, 41

Galsworthy, John, 71
Gambling, 65, 115, 116
General Film Company, 64
German American Bund, 70
Germany, 64, 70, 73
God's Little Acre, 185, 186, 187
Grauman, Sid, 163
Grauman's Chinese Theater, 163
Greed, 72
Grey, Nan, 73, 104
Gwynne, Anne, 91, 92

Havoc, June, 136
Hayward, Susan, 188–191
Hearst, William Randolph, 21, 22
Hecht, Ben, 130
Hepburn, Katherine, 68
Hers to Hold, 111
Hervey, Irene, 97
Hobart, Rose, 58
Hole in the Head, A, 194, 195
Hollywood, 69, 76
Hoodlum Priest, The, 159
Hope, Bob, 161
How the West Was Won, 156
How They Make a Motion Picture, 12, 61
How to Murder Your Wife, 196, 197
Howard, Lewis, 108

I Want to Live, 188, 189, 191
I'll Take Sweden, 161
Indians, 156, 169, 170, 178
Ingram, Rex, 160, 176
Invisible Man, The, 71, 158
It's a Date, 98, 108

Jean, Gloria, 61
Jewish Home for the Aged, 66
Johnny Guitar, 142, 143
Johns, Glynis, 155, 164, 165
Johnson, Lynda Byrd, 161
Johnson, Lyndon, 161
Jones, Allan, 35, 97

Karloff, Boris, 26–30, 68
Kelly, Gene, 111
Kern, Jerome, 73
Kirov, Ivan, 130, 131
Knox, Elyse, 90
Koster, Henry, 73

Laemmle, Carl, 25, 64, 65, 66, 67, 68, 69, 70, 71, 75, 76, 79, 114, 115, 116
Laemmle, Carl Jr., 67, 68, 79
Laemmle, Edward, 68
Laemmle, Rosabelle, 65, 66
Lanchester, Elsa, 30
LaPlante, Laura, 32
Laughton, Charles, 114
Laupheim, 64, 67, 68, 69, 70, 75
Lazlo, Bob, 158
Lehmann, Lotte, 66
Leica, 156, 157
Lemmon, Jack, 197
Levigard, Joe, 68
Levine, Nat, 114
Lisi, Virna, 196
Location, 117, 158, 159, 160, 161
Logan, Ella, 61
Lombard, Carole, 99, 100
Lord, Jack, 185
Louise, Tina, 186, 187
Loy, Myrna, 114

MacArthur, James, 186
Macbeth, 119, 150, 152, 153, 154
Mack Sennett Studio, 114
Man Who Laughs, The, 24
Mara, Adele, 149
Mascot Studio, 114
Mason, James, 114, 135, 136
Massey, Ilona, 127, 128
Mayer, Louis B., 17, 19
McDaniels, Hattie, 34
McDonald, Grace, 85
McHugh, Jimmy, 61
McRae, Henry, 24
Menjou, Adolph, 105, 157
Merry Go Round, 72
Merry Widow, The, 72
Milland, Ray, 98
Mission to Moscow, 20
Missouri State Prison, 159
Mitchum, Robert, 114
Montez, Maria, 76, 77
Moore, Constance, 82
Moore, Eva, 30
Moran, Peggy, 82, 83
Mowbray, Allan, 54
Muni, Paul, 17
Murphy, George, 61
Murphy, Maurice, 48
Murray, Ken, 136
Muse, Clarence, 12
My Little Chickadee, 62, 63, 72
My Man Godfrey, 99, 100

Nagel, Ann, 82
Napier, Alan, 119

Nazis, 70
Nazism, 73
Newman, Kurt, 69
Nice Girl?, 109
Night Life of the Gods, 54
Night of the Iguana, 159
Nolan, Jeanette, 119

O'Brien, Edmond, 110
O'Connor, Donald, 94
O'Herlihy, Dan, 119, 166
Old Dark House, The, 31
One Hundred Men and a Girl, 105, 156, 157, 171, 172

Paige, Robert, 106
Pallette, Eugene, 100, 105
Parrish, Helen, 104
Pasternak, Joe, 73
Patrick, Gail, 100
Patsy award, 163
Penner, Joe, 95
Photographers, 74, 116, 155, 156, 157, 159, 161, 162, 163
Pidgeon, Walter, 98
Pierce, Jack, 27
Plainsman and the Lady, The, 127
Powell, William, 99
Pratt, William, 68
Prisoner, The, 12
Property men, 158
Publicists, 74, 160, 161, 162, 163

Queen Kelly, 72
Queen Marie of Rumania, 161
Quiet Man, The, 118

Rage of Paris, The, 80, 81
Ralston, Vera Hruba, 117, 118, 146, 147, 148
Raye, Martha, 96
Realism, 72
Red Pony, The, 133
Reed, Barbara, 48, 73, 98, 104
Renavent, Georges, 57
Republic Studios, 114, 115, 116, 117, 118, 119, 130, 133, 136, 137, 142, 150
Resurrection, 161
Road Back, The, 48, 49, 50, 51, 52
Robeson, Paul, 34
Rodriques, Estalita, 125
Rogers, Roy, 114, 118, 163
Ross, Jack, 65
Russell, Jane, 144, 145
Ryan, Robert, 185

Sakall, S. Z., 106
San Fernando Valley, 24, 65, 69, 114, 117
Sands of Iwo Jima, 118, 120, 121
Sanford, Erskine, 151
Saroyan, William, 20
Schannon, Peggy, 54
Schayer, Richard, 79
Schildkraut, Joseph, 127
Schwartz, Maurice, 17–20
Security guards, 116, 117
Sennett, Mack, 114
Showboat (silent), 32, 34
Showboat (sound), 33, 34, 35, 36

Sinatra, Frank, 194, 195
Singing cowboys, 118
Sloman, Edward, 36, 37, 158
Spectre of the Rose, 130, 131
Spring Parade, 106
Stack, Robert, 109
Stern, Abe, 15, 23, 24
Stern, Julius, 15, 23
Stokowski, Leopold, 157, 171, 172, 173, 174
Stuart, Gloria, 31
Summerville, Slim, 51
Surrender, 36
Sutter's Gold, 55, 56
Swanson, Gloria, 138

Tamiroff, Akim, 106
Temple, Shirley, 73
That Certain Age, 107
Three Smart Girls, 73, 98, 103, 104
Three Smart Girls Grow Up, 104
Timberjack, 117
Top of the Town, 61
Tracy, Lee, 56
Trigger, 118, 163
Twentieth Century-Fox, 164

United Artists, 123, 161, 185, 188, 196
Universal City, 65
Universal Studios, 24, 25, 31, 32, 34, 36, 37, 46, 47, 54, 57, 61, 64, 66, 67, 68, 69, 70, 71, 72, 73, 74, 75, 76, 78, 79, 82, 96, 98, 100, 103, 106, 114, 156, 158, 162, 163
University of California, 71

Valentino, Rudolph, 68, 163
Van Every, Dale, 79
Veidt, Conrad, 25
Vincent, June, 86, 87
Von Stroheim, Erich, 16, 71, 72, 73

Wanger, Walter, 162
Warner Brothers, 17, 20
Waterloo Bridge, 53
Wayne, John, 114, 118, 119, 120, 121, 122, 123, 124
Webb, Jack, 192, 193
Webber, Peggy, 153
Welles, Orson, 114, 119, 150
Wells, H. G., 71
West, Mae, 62, 63, 72
Westerns, 70, 71, 114, 118, 156, 168, 177, 178, 179, 180, 181, 182, 183, 184
Whale, James, 70, 71, 158
White, Sammy, 33
Widmark, Richard, 161, 162
Wills, Bremmer, 31
Wills, Chill, 126, 127
Wilson, Charles, 56
Wilson, Harry, 161
Winninger, Charles, 36, 73, 85, 104
Withers, Jane, 73, 94
Wyler, William, 25, 68
Wynn, Keenan, 194

Yates, Herbert J., 114, 115, 116, 117, 118, 137
Young, Felix, 79
Young, Loretta, 101, 102